Reuniting looked after with their families

A review of the research

Available in alternative formats

Reuniting looked after children with their families

A review of the research

Nina Biehal

national
children's
bureau

Joseph Rowntree Foundation

The Joseph Rowntree Foundation has supported this project as part of its programme of research and innovative development projects, which it hopes will be of value to policy-makers, practitioners and service users.

National Children's Bureau

NCB promotes the voices, interests and well-being of all children and young people across every aspect of their lives. As an umbrella body for the children's sector in England and Northern Ireland, we provide essential information on policy, research and best practice for our members and other partners.

NCB aims to:
- challenge disadvantage in childhood
- work with children and young people to ensure they are involved in all matters that affect their lives
- promote multidisciplinary, cross-agency partnership and good practice
- influence government through policy development and advocacy
- undertake high-quality research and work from an evidence-based perspective
- disseminate information to all those working with children and young people, and to children and young people themselves.

The views expressed in this book are those of the authors and not necessarily those of NCB, the Joseph Rowntree Foundation or the Open University.

Published by the National Children's Bureau for the Joseph Rowntree Foundation

National Children's Bureau, 8 Wakley Street, London EC1V 7QE
Tel: 020 7843 6000.
Website: www.ncb.org.uk
Registered Charity number 258825

NCB works in partnership with Children in Scotland (www.childreninscotland.org.uk) and Children in Wales (www.childreninwales.org.uk).

© University of York 2006

Published 2006

ISBN 1 904 787 64 9

British Library Cataloguing in Publication Data
A catalogue record for this book is available from the British Library

Contents

Acknowledgements

I would like to thank the Joseph Rowntree Foundation, and in particular Susan Taylor and Anne Harrop, for supporting this project. I am also very grateful to Richard Barth, Roger Bullock and Elaine Farmer for their comments on the manuscript and to my colleague at the Social Work Research and Development Unit, Ian Sinclair, for his advice and support throughout. I would also like to thank colleagues at York University's Centre for Reviews and Dissemination, the Social Policy Research Unit and the Centre for Housing Policy for their helpful advice on the conduct of reviews.

Introduction

Background to the review

Family reunification refers to the rehabilitation of looked after children within their families. Prior to the Second World War, contact between separated children and their families was generally discouraged. In the early post-war years, Bowlby's influential work on the psychological consequences of separation for children raised concerns about children separated from their parents for lengthy periods (Bowlby 1951). In the USA Maas and Engler's study of children in long-term foster care was equally influential and led policy-makers and researchers to focus on the need to reduce the number of children in care (Maas and Engler 1959).

It was the Children Act 1948 that first emphasised the importance of reuniting children in care with their families. As the 1950s progressed, increasing numbers of children in the care system, the rising costs associated with this and, in the UK at least, pressure from social work professionals for wider powers to undertake preventive work, converged to focus attention both on the prevention of admission to care and on the rehabilitation of children separated from their families (Heywood 1978). These concerns contributed to the framing of the Children and Young Persons Act 1963, which was the first legislation to set out a statutory duty both to prevent the unnecessary admission of children to care and to rehabilitate them with their families wherever possible.

During the 1970s researchers highlighted the problem of children who 'drifted' in care as a result of a lack of proper planning and concern grew regarding the possible consequences of long-term care for the psychosocial development of children (Fanshel and Shinn 1978; Goldstein, Freud and Solnit 1973; Rowe and Lambert 1973). These concerns have formed one element of the continuing conflict between protagonists representing two value positions in childcare: the 'state as parent' and the 'kinship defenders' (Fox Harding 1991). Drift in care was of concern to protagonists in both camps and was used to lend weight both to arguments for more rapid decision-making regarding permanent placement away from home **and** for greater attention to prevention and rehabilitation.

In response to these concerns, the permanency planning movement emerged in the USA during the early 1970s and rapidly gained support in the UK, providing the impetus for attention to reunification. The permanency planning approach encouraged a focus on finding permanent homes for children in care. Rehabilitation with families was the placement of choice, but failing that, adoption or permanent foster care were recommended (Maluccio and Fein 1983). During the early 1970s UK researchers drew attention to the fact that, once children were admitted to care, social workers spent little time visiting their families and rarely planned for their futures (George 1970; Rowe and Lambert 1973; Thorpe 1974); in the UK the emphasis of permanency planning tended to be on finding permanent substitute families for children rather than on planned work to return them home.

As the 1970s progressed, public enquiries into the child abuse scandals in the UK helped to shift attention from prevention and rehabilitation. In any case, in this country there has tended to be a stronger emphasis on preventing entry to care than on efforts to rehabilitate children with their families once they have entered the care system.

A number of British research studies during the 1980s revealed that children continued to 'drift' in care for lengthy periods as a result of a lack of proper planning (Department of Health and Social Security 1985). For those who did return, the process was fraught with difficulties. As time progressed, social worker contact diminished and little attention was paid to preparation for children's return home. Return was rarely planned and often resulted from placement breakdown (Millham and others 1986; Thoburn 1980). During the 1990s, researchers continued to find a laissez-faire approach to return and a lack of proactive planning for the rehabilitation of looked after children (Bullock, Gooch and Little 1998; Farmer and Parker 1991).

With the passing of the Children Act 1989, there came a renewed emphasis on support to families to prevent the need for children to become looked after or to spend lengthy periods of time in care. However, relatively few British studies have focused on reunification. There have been, nevertheless, many studies of substitute care, some of which touch on the reunion of looked after children with their families and which can offer insights into this process. In contrast, there is a substantial body of research on family reunification in the USA. Numerous studies have sought to identify the predictors of reunification and there has also been small number of experimental studies of specialist family reunification services. The two bodies of research are quite different, with most British studies using qualitative methods to focus on process and most US studies using quantitative methods to describe and explain patterns of reunification. Studies from both countries have much to contribute to the development of policy and practice.

Policy and practice relevance

From a policy perspective, the reunification of looked after children with their families is a key issue in contemporary social care. The current government drive towards increasing rates of adoption for looked after children is also pertinent. This initiative has been met by counter claims that this policy risks depriving such children of continuing contact with their birth families. This may have additional ramifications for children who are black or of mixed ethnic origin (who are over-represented in the care system), who may lose contact with their communities as well as their families as a consequence of adoption. In this highly contested policy domain, it is vital that an alternative route to securing permanency for looked after children is not ignored, namely, the possibility of successful rehabilitation with birth families. In any case, adoption is unlikely to be an option for many older children, as the mean age at adoption is 4.5 years (National Statistics 2004). Reunification may offer older children their only chance of a permanent family home.

A further policy concern arises from the high costs of residential and foster care, and the current drive to raise standards in these sectors is likely to make such an option even more expensive. There had been a steady downward trend in the number of children looked after since the late 1980s, but this came to an end in 1994 when numbers started to rise. This has been attributed to the fact that, although fewer children now enter care, they stay longer. This trend has resulted in an increase of 14 per cent in the total number of days of care provided during the course of year in the period 1996–2000, which has inevitably led to increased pressures on local authority resources. There has been particular pressure on foster care resources, with a rise of 15 per cent in the volume of foster care provided over this period (Department of Health 2001; National Statistics 2003).

These resource pressures have contributed to a shortage of placements, and this reduces placement choice, making it more difficult for social workers to provide placements that meet children's individual needs. In view of the pressures on placement resources, the evidence that the state is not always a good parent, and the poor outcomes for those eventually leaving state care, it makes sense to explore the potential not only of preventive services but also of services to rehabilitate looked after children with their families.

However, reunification is not, in itself, self-evidently a safe policy. A recent Children Act Report has shown that the looked after system is increasingly populated by children who have been abused (Department of Health 2000). This raises important issues for family reunification. It may well be beneficial for some children to be reunited with their families, but it is important to consider carefully which children are likely to benefit. Crucially, it is important to consider whether children are likely to be at risk of re-abuse if returned home.

The indications are that family reunification continues to be a neglected area in both policy and practice terms but, in the context of financial pressures on the care system and the drive to increase adoption from care it is, in fact, a highly topical issue. This review offers an appraisal of the available research evidence on the reunion of looked after children with their families.

The review questions

The review will address three related questions:

1   Which factors are associated with the likelihood, and timing, of reunion for looked after children with their families?
2   How effective are specialist interventions designed to facilitate this reunion?
3   What are the outcomes of reunion for children?

Selection of studies

The review will include:

1   Studies that have addressed directly the question of family reunification since 1973, when concerns about 'drift' in care first came to the fore in both Britain and the USA.
2   Evaluations of specialist family reunification services, all of which have been developed in the USA.
3   Studies of children in substitute care in the UK that have addressed the issue of reunification within a wider remit. Only studies undertaken since the implementation (in 1991) of the Children Act 1989 are included in this group, as the service context has changed considerably since then.

The review protocol in Appendix 1 specifies the criteria by which studies are included in the review, both in terms of their relevance to the review question and their quality. The aim of this protocol is to avoid bias by making transparent the judgements that underpin the conduct of this review, so that decisions about those studies to be included and the quality of these studies are explicit (Centre for Reviews and Dissemination 2001).

The nature and context of the research evidence

Much of the evidence on reuniting looked after children with their families comes from the USA, but since there are differences in the child welfare systems of different countries, there are likely to be important differences in policy, practice and the nature of services. Findings from abroad raise important issues for consideration, but cannot necessarily be extrapolated directly to a UK context. Other important methodological issues arise as we consider specific questions in relation to reunification, such as the timing of return or the issue of ethnic origin, and these are discussed in the sections that follow.

In the context of the emphasis in the Children Act 1989 both on family support and on continuing parental responsibility, and given concerns about the high cost of looking after children, a preliminary question for any review of family reunification must be: how many children return home? However, the question of the numbers who return is only meaningful if we frame it as: how many return and **after how long**? Three months? One year? Ever? The answer is likely to differ according to the period of time under consideration.

This question of the timing of reunion itself begs a further important question: which factors are associated with the length of time that children remain looked after prior to reunion, or indeed, with whether they return home at all? It is this question that is addressed by the majority of studies on reunification. A number of studies of reunification have treated the duration of care as an evaluative criterion, for example studies of the effectiveness of specialist interventions designed to hasten reunification. Although the timing of reunion is a relatively straightforward concept, it has some limitations as a measure of the 'success' of the childcare system, because it assumes that exit from care is necessarily a good outcome. However, children may return home to unsatisfactory or abusive family situations, or they may repeatedly oscillate in and out of care.

Following a brief word of caution about the need to consider how different studies have gone about their investigations, this review begins with a discussion of what is known about the timing of reunion. Next, evidence on the relationship between child, family and service characteristics and patterns of return is examined. The review then considers whether specialist reunification services are effective in facilitating the earlier return of a greater number of children. This section focuses principally on the findings of the small group of experimental studies, all of them from the USA, that have addressed the topic of reunification. Finally, we turn to the question of the outcomes of return. How stable is the return home and which children are most likely to re-enter care following reunion? Importantly, what is the evidence on developmental outcomes for children reunified with their families and what is the risk of re-abuse for these children?

1. Making sense of the evidence on reunion

Before reviewing the research evidence on reunification, we consider briefly how the design of research studies included in this review can affect the evidence that such studies produce. For example, longitudinal studies that follow up children over time can answer different kinds of research questions compared to those that collect information at a single point in time. Similarly, studies that compare children to others with a different experience can answer different kinds of questions to those with single-group designs. Issues of research design such as these have an impact upon the claims that researchers are entitled to make on the basis of their investigations. If we fail to understand the basis on which studies of reunification have arrived at their results, we may draw misleading conclusions from their findings. Brief details of the studies referred to are therefore given in Appendix 2.

Sampling

Different studies of reunification have reported on samples of children who differ in important ways, and this can affect their findings. Some studies sample only children entering care for the first time in their lives, or only children placed under voluntary agreements, or only children entering foster placements, while others include children from a wider variety of circumstances. Some studies include all children entering the care system whereas others include only children looked after for, say, three, six or twelve months, and accordingly find that far fewer return. Children who remain in care for different periods of time may have different characteristics and circumstances, and these may affect the study findings.

To take just one example, differences in the age profiles of children sampled can bias findings and make comparison across studies difficult because, as we shall see below, age has been found to be one of the factors associated with the likelihood of return. Differences in the age ranges of children selected for study may, in turn, lead to variations in the proportion of children admitted for different placement reasons. A sample composed mainly of very young children is likely to include a higher proportion placed as a result of abuse or neglect and a lower proportion placed as a result of behavioural problems, than a sample which includes a substantial number of adolescents. As we shall see, there is some evidence that reasons for placement may be associated with the likelihood of reunion, thus sampling decisions of this kind may again affect findings on the probability, or timing, of return.

Also, depending on the way in which samples are selected, samples may or may not be representative of the wider population of looked after children. Researchers' attempts to generalise from small or unrepresentative samples should be viewed with some scepticism. However, studies with small samples may offer the best means of exploring issues in depth and gaining insight into complex circumstances and processes.

Definitions of reunification

Comparison between studies is further hampered by variations in the definition of reunification used. Some studies define reunion solely as a return to biological parents, whereas others consider that discharge from care placements to other relatives also constitutes reunion. With their broader definition of reunification, the latter are likely to report a higher proportion of children reunified than studies using a more restricted conceptualisation of return to a birth parent.

Sources of data

The source of the data will also have an effect on findings. Inevitably, there are problems with all sources of evidence but these vary, so it is helpful to bear in mind the particular limitations of the particular types of evidence used when considering the findings of studies.

Many of the studies from the USA derive their data from administrative databases containing information on thousands of children. Such large samples may give us some confidence that the study findings will be generalisable to other children, or at least those within the same country. Because movement in and out of care placements is associated with costs to the agency, it is likely that information on the duration of placements and the numbers leaving them will be reasonably accurate. These databases provide a very useful means of investigating the proportion of children who return home or re-enter care and the timing of discharge. However, in relation to other types of information that may be held on these databases, the information may not be a valid representation of a child's true circumstances. For example, the definitions used for 'disability', 'abuse' or 'behavioural problems' may vary according to who is using these concepts and who is entering the information.

Most importantly, agency databases exist for agency purposes, such as service planning and reporting to government, and typically contain only a limited range of information that is useful for the purpose of research. They may, for example, contain information about the time that children remain in care but not about why they leave. Many factors that might contribute to outcomes for children, such as the nature of parenting skills or the service provided, are usually absent. Thus, agency databases may be useful sources of information on which to base descriptions of children or processes but the restricted range of information they contain may limit the ability of researchers to explain the patterns they observe.

Studies drawing their data from social worker case records suffer from the same problems regarding the accuracy and validity of the information recorded as those who draw on agency databases, and because samples are necessarily smaller they may be less generalisable to other children. However, they are likely to contain much richer information on children, families, services and processes. Data from research questionnaires or interviews, on the other hand, may be gathered in a more consistent manner and cover a broader range of issues, although these are unlikely to have a 100 per cent response rate, and as with any other data source there may be some errors or missing data.

Type of analysis

Some quantitative studies of reunification have made claims about the correlates of reunification based solely on simple bivariate analyses, for example considering the relationship between contact and discharge from care without due attention to the other factors that may affect both of these. Analyses that fail to take account of the possible impact of other factors in this way may come to unwarranted conclusions, ignoring important markers such as the prior emotional or behavioural difficulties of children or reasons for placement when discussing outcomes. Research reports based on multivariate analyses, which take account of a wider range of variables, are likely to provide more convincing explanations for the outcomes observed.

2.   The timing of reunion

Assessing the evidence on the timing of reunion

The deceptively simple question of how many children are reunified with their families is not an easy one to answer because of considerable differences in the design of the studies that have addressed it. Studies using cross-sectional designs are based on 'snapshots' of a population of children looked after at a single point in time. Because many children enter care only briefly and rapidly return home, few of these will be 'captured' in cross-sectional samples of this kind. This kind of study design results in an over-representation of children who have been in placement for lengthy periods of time, some of whom are unlikely ever to return home, and an under-representation of those who leave care quickly. Such studies therefore suffer from a systematic bias, leading to overestimates of the length of time that children remain looked after.

The first UK study to raise the issue of 'drift' in care was Children Who Wait, which followed up a cross-sectional sample of children who had been looked after for a minimum of six months (Rowe and Lambert 1973). Indeed 75 per cent had been in care for two or more years and nearly half for at least four years. Consistent with later studies by other researchers, Rowe and Lambert argued that, after six months in care, the chance of return home diminishes considerably, and they expected that only around one in four would return home before school-leaving age. Yet their conclusions were in a sense tautological: they found that the majority in a sample of children who were **already** long-stayers were likely to remain looked after in the long-term.

Longitudinal studies that follow-up cohorts of **new** admissions to care are likely to provide more accurate estimates of the timing of return. The balance between short-stay and long-stay children in these samples will depend on the length of the follow-up period. However, even these studies may introduce bias in other ways. The influential US study Children in Foster Care found that after five years 56 per cent of a sample of new entrants to care had been discharged, in most cases to their own homes (Fanshel and Shinn 1978). Although this study analysed outcomes for a cohort of new admissions, children were included in the study only once they had been placed for 90 days, so these findings again refer to a relatively long-stay sample rather than to all children who enter care.

Furthermore, as a group, the children in this study were dissimilar to children entering care in the UK at that time. Children were only included in the study if they were under 13 years old on admission, had no disability and no history of offending. Analysis of a sample of 450 children who entered care in England at around the same time revealed that only one in eight of those entering care had similar characteristics to those in Fanshel and Shinn's study, raising questions as to whether their findings could be generalised to the UK (Millham and others 1986).

The duration of care episodes

National statistics

Similar problems arise in interpreting official statistics. Government statistics reveal that since the mid-1990s, the trend has been for decreasing numbers of children to enter public care. In 2001/2002, for example 24 per cent fewer children started to be looked after than in 1994/5 (DfES 2003). Despite this decline in the flow of children **entering** the system however, there has been an increase in the total number of children **in** the care system at any point in time (DfES 2003; DfES 2005). This is because those who do enter public care nowadays tend to stay longer. The proportion of children looked after for short periods (up to six months) has been declining and the proportion of those remaining for one year or more is increasing, as shown in Table 2.1 (Department of Health 2000; Department of Health 2001; DfES 2005).

It is important to note that the above figures refer to children ceasing to be looked after, not to children returning home. Although for those looked after for six months or less the two are likely to be synonymous, those placed for longer periods may exit for a variety of reasons, for example as a result of adoption or to ageing out of care in late adolescence.

A cross-sectional picture of the care population of this kind is likely to contain a disproportionate number of children who stay longer in care, because these long-stayers will have a better chance of being captured in a 'snapshot' on a single day.

Table 2.1: Duration of latest period of care for children who ceased to be looked after (2000–4; year ending 31 March)

Duration of care episode	Total children who ceased to be looked after (%)					
	1994	2000	2001	2002	2003	2004
Under 2 weeks	27	21	20	19	18	18
2–8 weeks	17	14	12	11	10	10
8 weeks–6 months	15	15	14	13	13	11
6 months–under 1 year	8	11	12	12	12	12
1 year–under 2 years	9	11	14	14	15	15
2 years or more	23	26	29	32	32	34

This trend towards longer periods of care can be more accurately discerned if we consider changes in the total period of time that children have been looked after since their last admission. Between 2000 and 2004, the average number of days of care per child rose by 19 per cent, indicating that the 'snapshot' figures given above do indeed reflect a real increase in periods of care (DfES 2005).

These trends are consistent with the increased emphasis on supporting children in their families since the implementation of the Children Act 1989. Those who enter care or accommodation after efforts to ensure their welfare within their families have failed are likely to stay longer. On 31 March 2004, for example, for 62 per cent of children looked after, the primary need for care was abuse or neglect. Reflecting this changing pattern, children are also increasingly likely to be placed under Care Orders rather than accommodated under voluntary arrangements (DfES 2005). The greatest increase in periods of care has been for those aged under five (20 per cent), followed by those aged five to nine (12 per cent). The trend since the mid-1990s has been for younger children to enter care, increasingly for reasons of abuse or neglect, and to remain longer as a result of the seriousness of their difficulties (Department of Health 2001).

To some extent these changes are the result of longer-term trends in reasons for admission to care. From the mid-1970s to the mid-1990s increasing attention to the prevention of placement, in tandem with growing concern about child abuse, led to a dramatic decline in numbers entering the care system overall, accompanied by continuing efforts to protect those children thought to be at risk of abuse. Another reason for the changing profile of the looked after population has been that, since the implementation (in 1991) of the Children Act 1989, Care Orders could no longer be made for reasons of offending. Prior to 1991 the care system had included a proportion of older children placed as a result of their involvement in offending, who in most cases had remained in placement for two years and then returned home. Today, young offenders are placed in secure units or young offenders institutions instead of in care placements, so younger children now constitute a higher proportion of the care population.

To sum up, an increasing proportion of all children looked after are younger children, many of whom are placed on court orders for reasons of abuse or neglect. In many cases, their problems are unlikely to be perceived as being amenable to rapid resolution and hence to early rehabilitation (Department of Health 2001).

Evidence from English studies

There have been relatively few longitudinal studies that have followed up children from the point of entry to care in order to report on numbers reunified and the timing of reunion. Findings from the main British studies that have explored this issue are summarised in Table 2.2.

As might be expected, Table 2.1 shows a pattern that is broadly similar to national statistics, with many children returning home quite quickly after admission but relatively few returning after six months have elapsed. In Bullock and colleagues' 1993 study, only a further 8 per cent of children separated from their families were reunited with them between two and five years after placement. This sample of children entered care in the early 1980s, while the children followed in the subsequent study by this team entered during 1993; the patterns identified are remarkably similar however. The pattern for the children in the Packman and Hall study shows fewer going home at an early stage which, although consistent with the national trend since 1994, is rather surprising as this study focused only on children accommodated on a voluntary basis. The study by Dickens and his colleagues,

Table 2.2: Proportion returning to parents or relatives (%)

Study*	Sample (n)	1 week	4 weeks	6 months	1 year	2 years
Bullock Little and Millham (1993)	450			58		77
Bullock, Gooch and Little (1998)	463	24	40	65	71	73
Packman and Hall (1998)	153		28	46		57
Dickens and others (forthcoming)	251		18	27		53

* Percentages for Bullock, Little and Millham (1993) have been calculated for the children who were actually separated from their families (n = 427) because some of the sample came to care but never left home.

conducted several years later, analysed data from 24 English authorities and found that, overall, fewer children returned home within one month and six months and more remained in long-term care, in comparison both with the other studies in this table and with national statistics.

The care careers of individual children may be affected not only by individual social work decisions but also by the operation of local care systems. Dickens and colleagues found that patterns of both placement and return vary considerably between local authorities and that early discharge is more common in authorities with lower thresholds for admission to care. They argue that in authorities with high thresholds for admission, children who do become looked after are likely to have very high levels of need and therefore a speedy return home is less likely (Dickens and others, forthcoming). A large study in the USA some years ago similarly came to the conclusion that the rate of discharge of children from care was related to the flow of children entering the system, with higher rates of entry accompanied by higher rates of discharge (Wulczyn 1991).

The declining likelihood of reunion

The relationship between time in care and the probability of a return home was first identified in an influential US study in 1959 (Maas and Engler 1959). The sample for this study included only children in care for at least three months. This meant that children placed long-term were over-represented, so their findings could not be generalised to a population of new entrants to care.

Since then, studies both in the UK and elsewhere have consistently found that the probability of reunification is greatest immediately following placement and that, statistically, the likelihood of discharge to either parents or relatives appears to decrease as time in care increases (Bullock, Gooch and Little 1998; Bullock, Little and Millham 1993; Courtney and Wong 1996; Courtney 1994; Finch, Fanshel and Grundy 1986; Goerge 1990; Millham and others 1986). For example, in the USA Finch and colleagues followed up a cohort of new entrants to care for two years. They found that, for children under one year old at placement, an increase of one year in the time in care was associated with a decrease of 40 per cent in the probability of a return to parents or relatives within two years (Finch, Fanshel and Grundy 1986).

Two studies by Courtney used a statistical method called event-history analysis to examine the impact of a variety of factors on the timing of exit from care for two random samples, each comprising over 8,000 new entrants to care in California.

Approximately 35 per cent returned to their families within a variable period of just over three years. Of those reunified, nearly half returned home within six months and 70 per cent within one year (Courtney 1994). The likelihood of reunification declined rapidly during the first five months after placement and thereafter it continued to decline very gradually (Courtney and Wong 1996).

In a much-quoted study, Goerge also used event-history analysis to chart how the probability of return changes as time progresses. Drawing a systematic sample of nearly 1,200 children who had entered care over a six-year period from an agency database in Illinois, he followed them up retrospectively for a further two years. All of the children studied had entered care for the first time. He found that the probability of reunification declined with the passage of time, but that this was true only for children placed for reasons of abuse or neglect, and not for those placed as a result of their emotional or behavioural problems or because their parents were unable to care for them. He also found wide variations in the timing of return associated with ethnic origin, region and placement type (Goerge 1990).

Duration of care as an explanatory concept

It seems clear both from official statistics and research that children are much more likely to return to parents or relatives shortly after placement than later on. The likelihood that they will return appears to decrease particularly sharply during the first few months after placement but much less rapidly thereafter. In the UK, the finding from the Lost in Care study that unless children returned home quickly (within six weeks) they had a very strong chance of still being in care in two years' time has entered the professional consciousness of social work (Millham and others 1986).

The widely disseminated Department of Health overview of a collection of government-funded studies, *Patterns and Outcomes in Child Placement*, emphasised that 'most of those who remain after six weeks are destined for a long stay' and highlighted the need for speed in reuniting children with their families (Department of Health 1991: 20). Although the consistency of these findings across studies indicates that these conclusions are likely to be true at a **descriptive** level, the issue of time in care has come to be been conceptualised as an **explanatory** variable as these research findings have passed into the received wisdom of many policy-makers and professionals. Thus, the misconception that remaining in care longer than six weeks, or six months, may in itself reduce a child's chances of reunification has become widely accepted.

This interpretation collapses factors such as the issues of delay resulting from a lack of purposeful planning by professionals, parental ambivalence, the reasons for placement and a variety of other potential factors into the notion that it is the passage of time that in itself diminishes the likelihood of reunion. The somewhat circular argument, which suggests that the longer children have been looked after, the greater the likelihood that they will remain looked after in the long-term, may well be true at a descriptive level but it does not offer an adequate explanation of the underlying reasons for this pattern. While it may be true that after around six months in placement, the longer a child is looked after, the smaller the likelihood of a return home, the duration of care episodes should be seen as a proxy for a variety of factors that may have contributed to this situation and not as the cause, in itself, of the failure to return.

A flavour of the different factors that may help to determine length of stay in care is given by two studies undertaken by the Dartington Research Unit (Bullock, Little and Millham 1993), both of which examined the factors associated with earlier or later return. The Going Home study included a five-year follow-up of 450 children first sampled in the earlier Lost in Care study (Millham and others 1986). It distinguished between three groups of children who returned home according to the length of time they were looked after. Over half of the separated children (52 per cent) returned to parents or relatives within six months of placement. These **'early returners'** were for the most part children under 12 years old whose families were temporarily unable to care for them. The most common reason for placement was parental illness (31 per cent of this group), followed by neglect or abuse (20 per cent) and the child's behaviour (19 per cent). Less than a quarter had been previously placed, so the majority did not appear to have entrenched difficulties. However 28 per cent of this group had returned to care within 12 months.

The **'intermediate returners'** – those who returned to parents or relatives between 6 and 24 months after placement – were predominantly adolescents removed from home as a result of either behavioural difficulties or family problems to which the children made a considerable contribution. Many came from ambivalent or rejecting families who failed to participate in their care and maintained only tenuous links with them.

The **'long-term returners'** – those who moved to parents or other relatives after two to five years in care – were the oldest group. Nearly four-fifths of this group had experienced abuse or neglect and in nearly half of the cases the child's behaviour was a contributory factor to their entry to care. These reunions of predominantly older adolescents were often negotiated informally between young people and relatives, sometimes in defiance of social work decisions. All of those who had not returned to relatives within five years (18 per cent) had poor links with parents. The findings from this study suggest that it was not so much time in care that was predictive of the likelihood of return but particular constellations of child and family problems and, associated with these, particular reasons for placement. Importantly, the quality of family relationships was one of the key variables predictive of the length of time in care.

A subsequent study by this team, Children Going Home, tested the variables identified in the earlier study on new prospective sample of 463 children (Bullock, Gooch and Little 1998). This study identified a cluster of factors that were predictive of return within six months. They found that there was a high probability of return where the child retained a role and territory within the family, the family considered itself as a family unit, the problems that led to separation had eased and the social work plan was inclusive. If all of these criteria were met, the odds of early return were found to be thirteen to one. The two largest groups of **early returners** were children looked after as a result of the hospitalisation of parents (although nowadays this is only rarely the reason a child becomes looked after) or adolescents placed for just a few days as a result of conflict with parents. The latter were usually short-term crises, often defused within a few days.

Return between 6 and 24 months after separation proved to be much harder to predict. Multivariate analysis showed that only two factors predicted 'intermediate return', namely that problems were felt to have been eased or resolved and that family relationships were reasonably good. Because problems often eased with the passage of time, the only factor shown to be of consistent value in predicting return outcomes after six months was the quality of family relationships.

These two studies reveal that the duration of care prior to the reunification of children with their families is related to a wide variety of factors. These may include the characteristics and attitudes of parents and children, reasons for placement and the characteristics of services. The chapter that follows this presents the research evidence on the factors associated with return.

Summary points

- Official statistics in England show that the trend since the mid-1990s has been for younger children to enter care, increasingly for reasons of abuse or neglect, and to remain longer because of the seriousness of their difficulties. In many cases their problems are unlikely to be perceived as being amenable to rapid resolution and hence to early rehabilitation.

■ The small number of longitudinal studies that have followed up children from the point of entry to care in the UK show a pattern that is broadly similar to national statistics, with many children returning home quite quickly after admission but relatively few returning after six months have elapsed.

■ Studies both in the UK and the USA have consistently found that the probability of reunification is greatest immediately following placement and that, statistically, the likelihood of discharge to either parents or relatives appears to decrease as time in care increases. However, evidence from a major study in the USA suggests that this may be true only for those children placed for reasons of abuse or neglect, and not for those placed as a result of their emotional or behavioural problems or because their parents were unable to care for them.

■ The fact that many children go home quite rapidly after placement has led to a common misconception that remaining looked after for longer than a few weeks or months may in itself reduce children's chances of being reunited with their families. This view collapses a variety of factors which may contribute to children remaining longer in care into the notion that it is the passage of time which diminishes the likelihood of reunion.

■ Some English studies have indicated that a variety of factors are related to the length of time that children remain looked after. These include the characteristics and attitudes of parents and children, the reasons for placement and the characteristics of services.

3. The probability of return: child and family characteristics

The factors that may contribute to the likelihood of return fall into three broad categories: those concerning the child, the family or the service provided. Other key issues that have been much discussed, and that overlap these three categories, include the reasons for placement and the impact of contact with parents while the child is placed. The impact of these factors is usually expressed either in terms of the **rapidity** with which children return home or the likelihood that they will be reunited with their families **at all**.

Only a few of the many studies that have explored these issues have addressed a wide range of possible factors. Naturally, the conclusions they come to regarding factors that predict longer, or shorter, stays in care will depend on the questions they have asked. Yet a review of 15 key US studies found that only six common predictors of time in care were investigated by as many as half of these studies, and only two of these predictors were consistently associated with time in care, namely, ethnic origin and parental contact (Glisson, Bailey and Post 2000). This review also found that inconsistencies in the results of different studies were sometimes a consequence of a failure to consider the interaction between different factors, for example age and reason for placement. Other critiques of the US research have highlighted the failure of many studies to take account of sibling groups who may enter and exit care at roughly the same time. Because outcomes for children in a sibling group will be related to each other, this results in double counting of the effects of belonging to a single family, leading to biased research findings (Guo and Wells 2003; Webster and others 2005).

Child characteristics

Numerous studies have explored whether the demographic characteristics of children, namely their gender, age or ethnic origin, make them more or less likely to return home after placement. To begin with, we can dismiss the impact of gender, which studies consistently have found **not** to be significantly associated with the likelihood of return (Albers, Reilly and Rittner 1993; Benedict and White 1991; Benedict, White and Stallings 1987; Bullock, Little and Millham 1993; Courtney and Wong 1996; Courtney 1994; Davis, Landsverk and Newton 1997; Finch, Fanshel and Grundy 1986; Goerge 1990; Stein and Gambrill 1977).

Age

There has been much discussion of whether age upon admission is associated with the likelihood of returning home. The picture that emerges across most of the studies that have addressed this issue is that children in middle childhood, around 4 to 12 years old, are generally more likely to return home than either infants or adolescents (for example, Courtney and Wong 1996; Courtney 1994; Fanshel and Shinn 1978; Fraser and others 1996; Glisson, Bailey and Post 2000; Grogan-Kaylor 2001; Harris and Courtney 2003; Kortenkamp, Geen and Stagner 2004; Wells and Guo 1999). One study found that both age and gender interacted with other factors predictive of return home and argued that this suggests that inconsistencies between study findings on these issues may be the result of not only differences in study samples but also of a failure to analyse the interaction of various factors (Glisson, Bailey and Post 2000). In general, though, the evidence from the USA suggests that 4–12 year olds are more likely to return to their families than younger or older children.

Other explanations for the variation in rates of return for different age groups may be related to the wider policy and practice context in both the UK and the USA. Professional perceptions of risk may vary in relation to different age groups. The options available to older and younger children may differ also. Other things being equal, one reason why younger children may be less likely to return home than remain in care may be because they have a greater chance of being adopted (Courtney and Wong 1996; Fein and others 1983). Older children who cannot return home are more likely to remain in care than be adopted, while adolescents may move to independence rather than return to their families. Also, adolescents who wish to leave placements may often vote with their feet, not only returning home of their own accord but also moving to stay with friends or elsewhere (Sinclair, Garnett and Berridge 1995).

The wider social and historical context at any given time may also be influential. For example, Courtney has written of the drug epidemic in the USA in the 1980s that resulted in the entry to care of many infants. He suggests that the difficulty of returning these children to drug-abusing parents may help to account for the fact that (US) studies at that time found infants were less likely to be reunified than older children (Courtney 1994). It is clear from this brief discussion that the association between age and the likelihood of return is far from simple and indeed, this is also the case for other factors associated with rates of reunification.

Ethnic origin

Virtually all of the available evidence on the relationship between ethnic origin and the rehabilitation of children with their families comes from the United States, but comparisons with ethnic groups in the UK are problematic. The largest group of children of minority ethnic origin who enter care in the United States are African-American, the second largest being children variously referred to as being of Latino or Hispanic origin. The latter group would have no obvious equivalent in the UK. In contrast, in England children of mixed ethnic origin constitute 8 per cent of those looked after (the same as the proportion of black children), but these do not figure to any great extent in US studies (DfES 2005). The discussion below will focus on comparisons in the North American studies between African-American and white children, since data on children of Hispanic origin is of little relevance to the UK.

Most US studies that have examined the relationship between reunification and ethnic origin have concluded that African-American children are less likely to return home than white children (Albers, Reilly and Rittner 1993; Courtney and Wong 1996; Courtney 1994; Courtney, Piliavin and Wright 1997; Davis and others 1996; Davis, Landsverk and Newton 1997; Fanshel and Shinn 1978; Glisson, Bailey and Post 2000; Goerge 1990; Grogan-Kaylor 2001; Harris and Courtney 2003; Jones 1998; Kortenkamp, Geen, and Stagner 2004; Lu and others 2004; McMurtry and Lie 1992; Seaberg and Tolley 1986; Wells and Guo 1999). Some studies have reported that African-American children are significantly less likely to return to their parents than white children, while others have expressed this in terms of a slower rate of return. For example, Wells and Guo (1999) found that, while the **rate** at which African-American children entered care was 98 per cent faster than for white children, they were reunified with their families 60 per cent slower than white children. McMurtry and Lie (1992) found that the likelihood that black children would return home was half as high for black as for white children, and that black children who did return had generally spent around twice as long in placement.

Only a few studies have found no relationship between ethnic origin and likelihood of reunification. The longitudinal study by Benedict and colleagues found no difference in the proportion of black and white children returning home to parents over a six-year period. The contrast with the studies cited above may possibly be the result of the much longer follow-up period used. Although other studies have indicated that black children return home at a slower rate than white children, differences apparent after only one or two years may even out over a longer period (Benedict, White and Stallings 1987).

Some have explored this issue further by examining the interaction of ethnicity with age, placement type, family structure and poverty. One study found that an interaction between age and belonging to an ethnic minority predicted a longer stay in care, but gave no information as to the nature of this age effect (Seaberg and Tolley 1986). Another reported that this interaction was only apparent among children who were not placed in kinship care, among whom black infants and teenagers returned home at a slower rate than white children but black children of other ages did not (Courtney and Wong 1996; Courtney 1994). However, this study also found that for those in kinship care placements, black children returned home at about half the rate for white children, irrespective of their age.

There has been some indication that family structure may also interact with ethnic origin. One recent study which examined the interaction of ethnic origin with family structure found that, while children from single-parent families were generally likely to return home at a slower rate than those from two-parent families, African-American children from single-parent families returned slowest of all (Harris and Courtney 2003). However, African-American children from **two-parent** families returned home at about the same rate as white children. They argue that because only 42 per cent of African-American families in the USA have two parents, compared to 77 per cent of white families, the interaction of ethnic origin and family structure may help to explain differences in reunification rates between children from different ethnic groups.

Poverty also appears to be a factor. Goerge found that, among a sample of children in their first care placements, black children living in an area of high economic disadvantage were likely to stay in care three times as long as white children, but this was not the case for black children from other areas. He concluded that it was children from poor black families who tend to stay in care longer, rather than black children from all socio-economic groups (Goerge 1990).

Associations with placement type have been examined too, as there is some evidence that the use of kinship care is particularly common for black children (Benedict, White and Stallings 1987; Berrick, Barth and Needell 1994; Grogan-Kaylor 2001; Landsverk and others 1996; Testa 1997), while the research on kinship care indicates that children in kinship care return home more slowly than those in other types of placements (see below). Grogan-Kaylor's analysis suggests that it is the interaction between these two factors that contributes to the fact that black children are less likely to return home, or do so more slowly. The limited evidence on this issue is mixed, however, as Courtney did not find that placement in kinship care contributed to the slower rate of return for black children (Courtney 1994).

Reflecting on these issues, Wells and Guo consider that ethnic origin may be a proxy variable for the way the child welfare system responds to black families, or the way that black families respond to the child welfare system, or for the particular stresses and resources of black families (Wells and Guo 1999). They conclude that perhaps it is the last of these that is most influential, observing that 'African-American status is confounded with poverty and single parent status and together they are linked to indicators of breakdown of community organisation and social control' (p.291).

However, great caution is needed in extrapolating from the pattern in the USA to the British context. It would be unwise to assume that we can at least compare black children in this country with black children in the United States. Certainly black families in both countries are likely to have much in common, namely their experience of racism, discrimination and, for a disproportionate number, poverty. Yet the social and historical contexts of their lives are potentially very different. While the experiences of black children in both countries may be similar in important ways, we cannot assume that the social context of their lives is equivalent and hence that patterns observed in the USA would necessarily be identical here. These findings do, however, suggest hypotheses that it might be useful to test in a UK setting.

Health and disability

A few studies have found that children with physical health problems tend to remain in care longer than those without. (Courtney 1994; Courtney, Piliavin and Wright 1997; Grogan-Kaylor 2001; Harris and Courtney 2003; Seaberg and Tolley 1986; Wells and Guo 1999). There is also some evidence from both English and US studies that children with disabilities are more likely to remain in care (Benedict and White 1991; Cleaver 2000; Courtney 1994; McCue Horwitz, Simms and Farrington 1994; McMurtry and Lie 1992; Seaberg and Tolley 1986). One US study found that having a disability decreased the probability that a child would leave care by 9 per cent (Glisson, Bailey and Post 2000).

Cleaver's four-year follow-up of children in foster care found that children without disabilities were three times more likely to return home than those who did have a disability. Of those with a physical disability, 70 per cent were still looked after four years after placement, compared with 38 per cent of those without a physical disability. However, the evidence is mixed, as Landsverk and colleagues' multivariate analysis of data on a large sample of children found that children with a physical disability were no less likely to be reunified than those without (Landsverk and others 1996).

Children with a learning disability appear to be especially likely to remain longer in care (Berridge and Cleaver 1987; Davis, Landsverk and Newton 1997; Seaberg and Tolley 1986). For example, Cleaver found that 67 per cent of children with a learning disability remained in foster care four years after placement, compared to 38 per cent of those without such a disability (Cleaver 2000). McCue Horwitz and her colleagues found, in a sample of children aged seven years or under, that those with developmental problems were less likely to have returned home (during a nine-month to five-year follow-up period). If they were also younger (age 2–5 years) and non-white they were even less likely to do so, as 85 per cent of children with this combination of characteristics remained in care compared to 44 per cent of those without them (McCue Horwitz, Simms and Farrington 1994). However, Landsverk's study of an older sample (aged 2–16 years), placed for a minimum of five months, found that variables which indicated developmental/learning problems were not significantly associated with reunification during an 18-month follow-up period (Landsverk and others 1996). The difference between this study and the two others mentioned may possibly be the result of differences in their sampling strategies and follow-up periods.

Emotional and behavioural difficulties

A US study of 669 children, which used multivariate analysis to examine the impact of psychosocial functioning on reunification, found that problems in psychosocial functioning significantly decreased the probability of reunification (Landsverk and others 1996). The impact of this was more marked for children in routine care placements than for those in kinship placements. This study followed up a cohort of new entrants to care for 18 months, but included only children placed for five months or more in their analysis. Using a standardised measure of emotional and behavioural problems, Achenbach's Child Behaviour Check List (CBCL), they found that children with externalising problems above the borderline cut-off point for clinically significant difficulties were half as likely to be reunified as were children below the borderline cut-point. However, high scores for emotional problems using this measure were not associated with reunification. The authors comment that only certain types of psychosocial problems have an impact upon decisions to return children home, namely the presence of especially troublesome behaviour.

A more recent US study has observed that, although the family factors precipitating many children's entry to care increases their vulnerability to mental health problems, most studies of the time that children spend in care have not assessed their emotional and behavioural problems. Among those that have, it has been unusual for researchers to use standardised research instruments recognised as valid measures of emotional and behavioural difficulties, such as the CBCL (Glisson, Bailey and Post 2000). They therefore used the CBCL to measure the internalising (emotional) and externalising (behavioural) problems of a random sample of 700 children age five years and over when they entered care (64 per cent) or youth custody placements (35 per cent).

Glisson and colleagues found that having emotional or behavioural problems decreased the probability that children would be reunited with their families. Adolescents with high scores for behavioural problems (above the cut-off point for clinically significant problems) were likely to remain longer in placement, whereas pre-adolescents with similar scores returned home more rapidly. There was also an interaction between child emotional problems and parental substance abuse, to the effect that children with this combination of circumstances were less likely to return home.

A few studies have found that children who experienced several placement moves are likely to remain longer in care (Davis, Landsverk and Newton 1997; Goerge 1990; Webster and others 2005). For example, Webster and colleagues found that children with three or more placements in care within a 12-month period were less likely to return home than those with two or less placements. Placement instability may in some cases be an indicator of emotional and behavioural difficulties, which may make reunion harder to achieve.

Family characteristics

Family composition

Several US studies have found that children from lone parent families, in most cases headed by mothers, are likely to return home at a slower rate than those with either two biological parents or one biological parent plus another parental figure (Courtney 1994; Courtney, Piliavin and Wright 1997; Davis and others 1996; Fraser and others 1996; Harris and Courtney 2003; Landsverk and others 1996). The difference in patterns of return appears to be quite marked, as two studies have found that those removed from a lone parent are three times less likely to return than those removed from two parents, even if only one of these parents is a biological parent (Davis and others 1996; Landsverk and others 1996), while another found that children from mother-only families were reunified at a rate 33 per cent slower than those from families with two parents (Wells and Guo 1999). Children from lone parent families have also been found more likely to be re-referred to social services after their return compared to those living with two parents (Jones 1998).

Children living with **neither** biological parent prior to placement appear to be the least likely to be reunified with their relatives (Courtney 1994). It is important to be clear that the issue here is one of return to these relatives, rather than to parents. One study found that they were three times less likely to return than those living with at least one biological parent (Landsverk and others 1996), while another reported that this group was reunified at a rate 48 per cent slower than those living with both their parents (Wells and Guo 1999).

Several English studies of the reunion of children with their families have also observed that in many cases families changed considerably while children were in placement (Bullock, Gooch and Little 1998; Farmer and Parker 1991; Fisher, Marsh and Phillips 1986). Sometimes children who returned home subsequently had a number of moves among parents, extended family and friends. In their 1991 Trials and Tribulations study, Farmer and Parker found that younger children placed for reasons of abuse or neglect generally did best after their return when there had been no change in the household, or when there had only been a change in the parent's partner, and did least well when there had been a change in the children in the household.

A US study of sibling groups placed at the same time found that children placed with siblings were more likely to be reunited with their families within a 12-month period than those placed apart from one another. Surprisingly, the size of sibling group had no effect on the probability of reunion (Webster and others 2005).

Parental problems

The nature of parental problems also appears to be associated with the likelihood of return, although there is relatively little evidence on this issue. Not surprisingly, families with comparatively fewer problems and more personal resources are more likely to be re-unified than those with more, or more complex, problems (Fraser and others 1996). Parents with emotional problems, chronic mental illness or involved in offending may be less likely to have their children returned to them (Rzepnicki, Schuerman and Johnson 1997), and this has also been found to be the case for those with housing problems or who are homeless (Jones 1998; Rzepnicki, Schuerman and Johnson 1997).

Parental drug abuse has been highlighted as an important factor that reduces the likelihood of reunification (Jones 1998; Rzepnicki, Schuerman and Johnson 1997). However, one study found that children placed as a result of allegations of parental drug use returned twice as fast as those placed for other reasons. Importantly, children whose parents completed drug treatment programmes were reunified more than six times faster than children whose parents who were not drug-dependent (Smith 2003). However, completion of drug treatment was associated with faster reunification even when parents reported ongoing drug use or there were continuing concerns about high-risk parenting. Smith suggests that social workers may prioritise factors that are easier to measure, such as the completion of drug treatment, over those that are more difficult to measure, such as an improvement in parenting skills. There is also some evidence from another study (albeit with a sample of only 16 children), that children of parents who undertook treatment for substance abuse in the three months following the child's return home were more likely to re-enter care. The authors argue that parents with substance abuse histories who are actively seeking treatment may be less likely to provide a safe environment for their children than those not seeking such treatment. They urge caution when considering the return of children to substance-abusing parents (Miller and others, forthcoming).

Poverty has also been identified as a problem associated with a reduced likelihood of reunification (Barth and others 1987; Fraser and others 1996; Goerge 1990; Jones 1998). For example, a US study found that children from poor families returned about half as fast as children whose families' income was above the state poverty line (Smith 2003). Children from families living on state benefits or low incomes appear to be not only less likely to return home but also less likely to be adopted (Albers, Reilly and Rittner 1993; Courtney and Wong 1996).

Summary points

■ Research in the USA has shown that children in middle childhood (roughly, 4 to 12 year olds) are more likely to be reunited with their families than infants or adolescents. This may be the result of variations in professional perceptions of risk in respect of different age groups, because different options are available to infants and to adolescents (for example, adoption or independence), or because of the reasons for which children of different ages are placed.

- There is no evidence that gender is related to the likelihood of reunion.

- The evidence on the relationship between ethnic origin and patterns of discharge comes from the USA. Studies there have concluded that African-American children are reunited with their parents at a slower rate than white children. The reasons for this are complex. While these findings raise questions that should be explored in the UK, they cannot be directly extrapolated to this country.

- There is some evidence from both England and the USA that children with disabilities tend to remain longer in public care, particularly those with learning disabilities.

- Two major US studies have found that children with more severe emotional and behavioural difficulties are less likely to be reunited with their families.

- US studies have found that children from lone parent families are likely to remain longer in public care. One study also found that those living with neither of their biological parents prior to placement were the least likely to return to live with either parents or other relatives.

- English studies have consistently found that the composition of the families of looked after children often changes significantly while they are being looked after. The particular ways in which families have been reconstituted during a child's absence may affect the likelihood of a harmonious return.

- US studies have found a variety of parental problems to be associated with a lower probability of reunion, including poverty, parental drug misuse and chronic mental illness.

4. Placement reasons, contact and motivation

Reasons for placement

A number of studies have suggested that the rapidity with which children are reunited with their families may be associated with the reasons which have led them to become looked after. There is some evidence that children placed under voluntary arrangements may return to their families more rapidly, presumably because fewer of them are likely to have severe difficulties than those placed under statutory arrangements. In England, Cleaver found that these children were three times as likely to be rehabilitated with their families as those placed under care orders. (Cleaver 2000). Some children entering care under voluntary arrangements may be placed as a result of a family crisis and children admitted during a crisis may return home relatively quickly because it is in the nature of crises that they subside after a time (Fraser and others 1996; Seaberg and Tolley 1986).

Parental illness

The most common family crisis associated with early reunification has been a parent's physical illness. Two English studies found that just under one-third of those who returned home within six months had been placed as a result of a parent's illness, while a US study of children placed for 90 days or more found that those who had entered care as a result of parental illness were more likely to return home within one year than other children (Bullock, Little and Millham 1993; Fanshel and Shinn 1978). Bullock and colleagues' prospective study found that 32 per cent of those who returned home within six months had been placed as a result of the hospitalisation of parents (Bullock, Gooch and Little 1998). Cleaver's study of English children in foster care for three months or more found that those whose reason for placement was related to a parent's physical illness were almost twice as likely to returned home (65 per cent) as those placed for other reasons

(37 per cent), while a study in the USA found that children whose mothers were in poor health at the time of placement were four times as likely to be reunified with them as other children (Cleaver 2000; Kortenkamp, Geen and Stagner 2004). However, in recent years only 6 per cent of children placed have been in need as a result of a parent's illness or disability, so this placement reason will account for the timing of return for relatively few of those reunited with their parents (DfES 2005).

Child behaviour problems

Children whose entry to care is related to their behavioural problems appear to be reunified more quickly than those entering as a result of abuse, neglect or parental problems. A US study of 886 families found that problems that were child-centred were more common among those reunited, whereas problems that were parent-centred were more common among families who were not reunited. Children whose placement was related to parent–child conflict, relationships with peers or siblings, school academic problems or school behaviour problems were more likely to be reunited than those whose parents had emotional or problems, or problems of drug abuse, chronic mental illness, offending or homelessness (Rzepnicki, Schuerman and Johnson 1997).

Other studies in both the USA and UK have found that children placed for behavioural problems (Bullock, Gooch and Little 1998; Fanshel and Shinn 1978; Glisson, Bailey and Post 2000; Vernon and Fruin 1986), 'child-related reasons' (Fraser and others 1996) or 'status offences', such as running away (Lewandowski and Pierce 2002), were more likely to return home, or to return sooner, than those placed for abuse or neglect.

Abuse and neglect

The picture that emerges from most studies which have examined the impact of placement reasons on patterns of reunification is that children placed for reasons of abuse or neglect are likely to remain longer in care than those placed for other reasons (Cleaver 2000; Davis and others 1996; Fanshel and Shinn 1978; Landsverk and others 1996). Studies which have considered the impact of abuse and neglect separately upon patterns of reunion have, in most cases, found that children placed as a result of physical or sexual abuse are likely to return home more quickly than those placed for neglect.

Most studies which have examined this issue have found that children placed as a result of neglect are reunified more slowly than those placed for other reasons (Courtney and Wong 1996; Courtney, Piliavin and Wright 1997; Davis, Landsverk and Newton 1997; Glisson, Bailey and Post 2000; Harris and Courtney 2003; Kortenkamp, Geen and Stagner 2004; Webster and others 2005). Davis and her colleagues found that those placed as a result of neglect were likely to remain in care five times longer than children who had not experienced this.

More specific comparisons have also been made. Some studies have reported that those placed for neglect are more likely to remain in care than those placed for physical abuse (Wells and Guo 1999) or either physical or sexual abuse (Grogan-Kaylor 2001). In his eight-year follow-up study of over 1,000 children entering care in Illinois Goerge examined the changing patterns of return over time for children placed for different reasons, although he did not distinguish between placement as a result of physical or sexual abuse. He found that while abused children are likely to return home more quickly than children who have experienced neglect, some abused children never return home because of the continuing risk of re-abuse. In contrast, although children placed as a result of neglect are likely to remain longer in care, he found that most did return home eventually (Goerge 1990).

The English Trials and Tribulations study, which reported that physically abused children were likely to return home sooner than those placed as a result of neglect, found that this was largely a result of the fact that active plans for reunion were more frequently made for those who were placed as a result of physical abuse than for those placed as a result of neglect (Farmer and Parker 1991). The severity of the abuse is likely to be a consideration here. Barth and his colleagues' study of a sample of physically abused children found that children were more likely to return home where abuse was less severe, in comparison with those who had experienced more severe abuse. They hypothesised that this may be because social workers give more attention to reunification efforts with families where there appears to be a greater chance of success (Barth and others 1987).

As for sexual abuse, two studies have indicated that children placed as a result of sexual abuse are returned to their families relatively soon in comparison with those placed for other reasons. Davis and colleagues reported that they were two-and-a-half times more likely to be reunited with their families if placed as a result of sexual abuse, compared to those with no evidence of sexual abuse (Davis and others 1996). Similarly Landsverk and his colleagues found that those placed as a result of sexual abuse were three times more likely to return to their families than those without evidence of this form of abuse and those placed for emotional abuse were two-and-a-half times more likely to do so (Landsverk and others 1996). More specifically, Courtney found that sexually abused children were more likely to return home than those placed as a result of neglect (Courtney 1994). This is likely to be because the risk of sexual abuse may diminish rapidly if the perpetrator leaves the home, whereas neglect is often chronic.

Contact

The fact that looked after children are likely to benefit from continuing contact with their families has rarely been contested. Many writers have pointed to the benefits of preserving the parent–child relationship, drawing on attachment and other theories to argue that this is important for children's sense of identity and belonging, their ability to develop other attachments, their mastery of developmental tasks and their ability to cope with the stress of separation and placement (Davis and others 1996; Hess and Proch 1988; Maluccio, Pine and Warsh 1994; Millham and others 1986). There are also pragmatic reasons for encouraging contact, where this is not harmful to the child. As we saw earlier, many children do eventually return to live with their families, although these families may have been reconstituted by the time they return. Also, among those who leave care when they are 16 years old or over, a small proportion return home initially while others look to their families for support when living independently, so the preservation of ties to their families of origin may be helpful in the longer term (Biehal and others 1995).

However, when thinking about contact it is important to be clear about **who** children desire contact with and who it is beneficial for them to be in contact with. Where contact with a parent is considered detrimental, contact with siblings or other relatives may be particularly important. Also, as Schofield has observed, it is important to understand children's expressed desire for contact, or apparent lack of interest in it, in the context of the maltreatment or separation they have experienced, which may have developmental consequences for them. Anxiety and confusion about proximity to a parent may lead them to develop strategies for survival, such as overly effusive or cool and distant behaviour towards a parent, which make it hard for practitioners to interpret the true nature of the parent–child relationship and to decide whether or not contact is beneficial for the child (Schofield 2005).

In a perceptive review of the empirical evidence on contact, Quinton and his colleagues have suggested that many of the arguments for contact between looked after children and their parents are concerned with the **rights** of children and birth parents, but attempts are often made to support these arguments by appeals to the research evidence on the **effects** of contact (Quinton and others 1997). Yet although much has been written on the importance of contact in promoting reunification, this literature largely takes the form of essays reflecting on the topic, and there have been few empirical studies of this issue. The conclusions of a small number of influential studies conducted during the 1970s and 1980s have led to the widespread acceptance that a lack of parental visiting may diminish the likelihood that children are rehabilitated with their families.

However, the relationship between contact and reunification is less straightforward than it might at first seem. A closer look at the evidence on contact reveals that, in some respects, the situation is similar to that regarding the impact of time in care on patterns of return, discussed earlier. On the basis of research findings showing that children who remain in care in the long-term had less parental contact than those who returned home after briefer placements, it has become widely accepted that contact is a causal factor in the timing of reunification. Again, a description of a bivariate relationship which is true at a **descriptive** level has been widely interpreted as being an **explanatory** concept. Yet there is little clear evidence that it is contact in itself that brings about reunification, although it may certainly be an important contributing factor.

The evidence on contact

The first major study to focus on this issue, Children in Foster Care, was a follow-up of 624 under-13 year olds newly admitted to care in New York, who remained in care for a minimum of 90 days (Fanshel and Shinn 1978). This study found that the proportion of parents visiting their children declined over a five-year period and that two-thirds of the children who received no visits during their first year of placement were still in care five years later. Given the accumulation of non-visited children in long-term care, the authors concluded that contact was a major determinant of whether children returned home, implying that contact could in some way **cause** reunification.

Yet in this study, multivariate analyses showed that parental visiting was also correlated with the caseworkers' own contact rate, their evaluation of the mothers and with child behaviour as well as with reunification. In fact, these were the strongest predictors of reunification. Contact was only one of a number of factors predictive of a return home. The correlation between contact and return home was strongest during the first six to nine months after placement, but subsequently its impact was far less marked. As Quinton and colleagues have commented, over the five-year follow-up period the only consistent predictors of reunification were the social workers' evaluation of the mother and the caseworkers' own contact rate (Quinton and others 1997). This may have been because caseworkers concentrated their reunification efforts upon families they perceived as offering better parenting: they may have offered more support to these mothers to facilitate visiting, or alternatively they may have evaluated them more positively **because** they visited regularly. Despite Fanshel's assertion in an earlier study that contact was the key to discharge, Quinton and colleagues concluded that it was only one of a number of variables which predicted a return home.

It has also been observed that the main source of change leading to discharge home in this study was change in family's capacity to care for child, which occurred in respect of 64 per cent of the children who returned home (Goerge 1990). However, the findings of this study refer only to children who were placed for a minimum of three months, and may not apply to children with other characteristics or circumstances.

More influential in the UK was the Lost in Care study, a prospective study that followed up 450 children of all ages over two years (Millham and others 1986). This found a strong bivariate association between contact and an early return home (within six months) and reported that barriers to contact between children and parents were more common among children placed for longer periods. Three-quarters of those who returned to parents or relatives within six months had regular contact with a parent. Yet the authors also state that for 57 per cent of this group, the reasons for an early return home stemmed from alterations to the family situation (for example, in health or the family environment), rather than changes in the behaviour of the children or parent. The majority of this group of 'early returners' had been admitted as a result of parents' temporary health or social problems and returned once these crises were resolved. Those who remained in care for more than six months were mainly abused or neglected children who tended to be older and often had behavioural problems. This suggests that child and parent psychosocial problems prior to admission to care were highly influential and it is clear that contact was only predictive of reunion for those reunited within six months of placement.

A follow-up of the Lost in Care sample in a subsequent study found that the reunion of 38 per cent of the 'early returners' was unsuccessful and the authors reflected that 'regular contact in itself cannot solve the problem' (Bullock, Little and Millham 1993: 91). In a further study by some members of the same team, multivariate analysis of data on a new prospective sample found that the variable 'contact' derived its predictive power from five others that were predictive of early reunion: the child's retention of both a role and territory within family, the family's perception of itself as a family, the inclusiveness of the social work plan and the easing of problems that led to separation (Bullock, Gooch and Little 1998).

Two earlier UK studies also observed that the longer children remained in care the less likely they were to be visited by their parents, although tests of statistical significance were not reported by either of them (Aldgate 1980; Rowe and Lambert 1973). Aldgate suggested that the maintenance of contact was a significant factor in influencing the return of children from care, but she argued that reasons for placement and the presence of purposeful social work activity were also influential. So although contact appeared to be important, it was not the only factor related to the rehabilitation of children. The Trials and Tribulations study also found that, for older children who were often placed as a result of their behaviour, continuing family contact was associated with successful rehabilitation, although purposeful case planning on the part of social workers was also an important ingredient in rehabilitation (Farmer and Parker 1991). In contrast, another English study of older children in residential placements found no evidence that those who had been in care longer had less frequent contact with their families than others (Sinclair and Gibbs 1998). Nearly two-thirds of these young people said they saw their families as much as they wanted to but just over one-third said they did not see them enough. Most wanted contact with their families on leaving care, but not a return home.

In the USA, Seaberg and Tolley reported that children visited more often spent less time in care (Seaberg and Tolley 1986). However, they cautioned that the impact of contact on the duration of time in care was only weak (accounting for only 0.116 of the variance) and that child characteristics and reasons for placement were also predictive of time in care. More recently Davis and her colleagues examined the relationship between parental visiting and reunification for a sample of 865 children aged 12 years or under, who were admitted to care for between 72 hours and 18 months and for whom there was a reunification plan (Davis and others 1996). At a bivariate level, both maternal and paternal visiting at the level recommended in court-ordered case plans were strongly associated with reunification. Multivariate analysis indicated that maternal visiting was the strongest predictor of reunification, indicating that a child visited by a mother at the recommended level was approximately ten times more likely to be reunified. Children were less likely to return if mothers visited less than at the recommended level. Other important predictors were being white, living with two parents (at least one of whom was a biological parent) and being removed from home as a result of sexual abuse.

Virtually all of these placements were court-ordered rather than voluntary, and visiting plans were stipulated by the courts. This may explain the strong association between levels of visiting and reunification. It seems that a failure to visit at the stipulated level led to the court's refusal to return children to their parents. However 44 per cent of those with maternal visiting plans and 38 per cent of those with paternal visiting plans were not reunited. The authors suggest that in these cases, reunification might always have been in doubt and that the visiting stipulation may have been made mainly to test parents' resolve to have their children back. In these circumstances, the court's recommendation of parental visiting may have been made as a form of evidence-gathering rather than as a therapeutic tool. They caution that if the aim is to encourage visiting in order to promote improved relationships, this is likely to require caseworkers' time and therapeutic skill.

The nature of contact

Although contact with families is likely to be beneficial to many children for the reasons outlined earlier, the impact of parental visiting on outcomes for children is likely to depend on the nature and quality of that contact. A note of caution has been sounded by one recent English study of children in foster placements, which found that the only variable which predicted re-abuse was weekly contact with a relative, irrespective of whether children returned home. Re-abuse was significantly more likely if no-one was forbidden contact with the child (Sinclair and others 2005).

In her analysis of qualitative data on 33 children in foster placements, most of whom were aged 5–12 years and placed as a result of abuse or neglect, Cleaver explored the relationship between contact and reunification (Cleaver 2000). One-third of these children had returned home by one-year follow-up. Cleaver found that contact was an important ingredient of return if it was purposeful, had the aim of improving the parent–child relationship and was a positive experience for the child. Contact helped to promote reunification in circumstances where parents were well motivated, actively participated in the return process and were willing to change and seek help. Contact was helpful where it was resourced and supported by social services, the return process taken at a steady pace and regularly re-assessed, and both parent and child were involved in the planning process. Parental visiting was also more helpful in promoting reunification if there was a good attachment relationship between parent and child. In her broader survey of contact, Cleaver rated the quality of attachment on the basis of information derived from 152 case files and found that the weaker the attachment, the stronger the likelihood that contact would be broken. This study highlighted the importance of a rigorous assessment of children's needs and parenting capacity prior to reuniting families and the importance of direct work with children and families to improve relationships.

A quantitative study of 75 children discharged from care in the USA came to similar conclusions (Milner 1987). There was a strong correlation between frequent, 'positively oriented' visiting and short-term placement. Through an analysis of case files, the author constructed a measure of the quality of relationship with birth family members, based on the frequency and nature of parental visiting. He found that a strong relationship between parents and children during placement was associated with a shorter time in care (explaining 28 per cent of the variance in duration of care). Social work activity with parents during placements was also correlated with early discharge. The author concluded that children who spend shorter periods in care are likely to be those who are visited frequently by their parents and for whom the parent–child relationship is positive.

In contrast, Hess and Proch argued that it was not the frequency of visits but their duration that was beneficial to children, finding that the duration of visits was related to the child's adjustment (Hess and Proch 1988). It is possible that the time that parents and children spent together on these occasions was an indicator of how positive their relationships were. Some have also warned that frequency of visiting should not be taken as a test of the depth of parents' attachment to their children, because parents may find visiting stressful, may feel unwelcome at the child's placement or bereft of a role, or may fail to visit because they feel angry, guilty or inadequate (Millham and others 1986; Rowe and Lambert 1973). The relationship between patterns of contact, parent–child relationships, child well-being and reunion is clearly a complex one.

It is clear from the research on contact and reunification that children who are regularly visited by parents and for whom this contact is a positive experience are likely to be those who remain in care for shorter periods. However, the evidence does not indicate that it is parental visiting in itself that brings about early reunion but rather that frequent parental visiting indicates the presence of a number of other factors. These may include a positive relationship and strong attachment between parent and child, parental motivation, placement for reasons such as parental ill health or other crises rather than serious and persistent parenting problems, support to parents from social workers and purposeful, planned social work activity. It seems likely from the evidence that it is this cluster of positive factors, including regular parental contact, which together are associated with the reunion of children with their families.

Motivation and ambivalence

Some of the research on contact suggests that motivation or ambivalence on the part of both parents and children may have some impact upon the probability of reunion. A small number of other studies have, either explicitly or implicitly, also touched upon this issue. Evidence from two studies of the effectiveness of specialist reunification services suggests that reunification may be more likely where parents were motivated to change their behaviour and to work towards reunion with social workers. The Alameda Project found that reunification was significantly less likely where parents were unwilling to sign contracts with workers (Stein and Gambrill 1977). This specialist service tested parental motivation to resume the parenting role through requiring their participation in planned activities to accomplish this.

The importance of parental motivation to work towards the return of their children was also indicated by the study of the Family Reunion Service (FRS), where workers reported that successful rehabilitation was more likely in cases where parents 'wanted to change' (Pierce and Geremia 1999).

In the UK, as mentioned above, Cleaver found that parental motivation and willingness to change contributed to successful return. Another study of children in foster care also highlighted the importance of parental motivation in relation to the successful rehabilitation of children (Sinclair and others 2005). Earlier British studies found it was often parents or older children who decided on reunion and sometimes took matters into their own hands. In the In and Out of Care study, whose sample was largely composed of teenagers, families often became concerned about the laxity of children's homes and about the inability of foster carers to enforce boundaries, and came to the view that it would be better for their children to return home. Others were motivated to take their children back by the view that their children were behaving better or had matured and that return would therefore be trouble-free (Fisher, Marsh and Phillips 1986). Similarly, Captive Clients, a qualitative study of children reunited with their families, found that parental determination to have their children returned to them was the most important factor in determining whether children went home (Thoburn 1980). Both this study and Trials and Tribulations focused on children who went 'home on trial' and both found that parent or child insistence on reunion often provoked the return, often in the absence of clear plans on behalf of social workers (Farmer and Parker 1991).

A few other studies have found either an apparent lack of parental motivation or parental ambivalence to be related to a failure to reunify families. A study of the implementation of care orders reported that plans for rehabilitation were sometimes abandoned where parents withdrew from assessment or it was felt that they were not making enough progress (Harwin and others 2001). As mentioned earlier, the parents of children in the Going Home study who remained in care longer than six months were reported to be often rejecting or ambivalent, and as time passed the children remained in care increasingly because of parental incapacity or indifference (Bullock, Little and Millham 1993; Millham and others 1986). This research team's intensive study of a later sample also observed that one of the reasons that children who were expected to return did not do so was ambivalence on the part of parents and/or children (Bullock, Gooch and Little 1998)

Only one study identified focused directly on parental ambivalence about reunification. In a qualitative study of 40 families whose children returned home but later re-entered care, researchers judged whether or not the parents had consistently wanted the child returned, or whether they appeared ambivalent about the situation, by means of an analysis of case records and interviews with parents, children and professionals (Hess and Folaron 1991). They concluded that, in many cases, parents had appeared ambivalent about their children's return. Parental ambivalence appeared to be connected to the parents' own childhood experiences, their personal problems and their lack of social support. A number of these ambivalent parents also had learning disabilities. In some cases, qualities in the children (for example, temperament, behaviour or disability) contributed to parental ambivalence, although it was difficult to determine whether behavioural problems themselves developed as a consequence of parental ambivalence. A problem with this study is that the sample was drawn on the basis of outcome, that is, the families selected were those for whom reunification had broken down. It cannot tell us whether any parents in families successfully reunified were also ambivalent about the return of their children and what it was that prevented these situations from breaking down also.

The reasons for parental ambivalence are likely to be complex. They may be connected to the strength of the parent–child relationship, the severity of parents' problems and the extent of social support available to them. Qualities in the child may also make them more difficult to care for and it has been suggested that the child's response to parental visiting may be a crucial factor, that is, whether a child is welcoming, hostile or apparently indifferent (Rowe and Lambert 1973). Children too may demonstrate reluctance or ambivalence about a return home as a result of earlier abuse or neglect; they may feel anxious, angry or fearful, or may feel torn between a sense of loyalty to their birth families and a reluctance to return to them. These are areas that have received little direct attention from researchers. The evidence on the link between parental motivation or ambivalence and the reunification of children is not strong but the (limited) research findings available suggest that this is an area worthy of further exploration.

Summary points

- Children placed as a result of parental illness are likely to be reunited with their families quite quickly. However, fewer children are placed for this reason today than in the past.
- Children whose entry to care is related to their behavioural problems are likely to return home more rapidly than those placed as a result of abuse, neglect or parental problems.
- Studies in both the UK and the USA have found that children placed as a result of physical or sexual abuse are more likely to return to their families than those placed for neglect. However, one study found that although children placed for neglect tend to remain longer in care, most do eventually return home, whereas a higher proportion of abused children never return home. Children who have been sexually abused are likely to return home soonest, perhaps because the risk to them rapidly diminishes if the perpetrator is removed from the home.
- Although many claims have been made as to the importance of continuing family contact in hastening the reunion of children with their families, there is relatively little research evidence on the effects of contact. There is no evidence that it is contact itself which leads to reunification, but some evidence that it is related to other factors predictive of return.
- The evidence suggests that frequent parental visiting indicates the presence of a number of other factors. These may include a positive relationship and strong attachment between parent and child, parental motivation, placement for reasons such as parental ill health or other crises rather than serious and persistent parenting problems, support to parents from social workers and purposeful, planned social work activity. It seems likely from the evidence that it is this cluster of positive factors, including regular parental contact, which together are associated with the reunion of children with their families.
- Evidence from a small number of studies suggests that parental motivation and parental ambivalence are associated with the likelihood of reunion. Ambivalence on the part of the child may have a similar effect.

5. The nature of services

Most of the research findings on the link between the social work services provided and patterns of reunion are concerned either with the issue of planning or with the effects of two broad types of placement, namely kinship care versus non-relative care.

Failure to plan for return

Failure to plan for looked after children has been a major theme in research on family reunification in the UK, which has been explored mainly through qualitative studies of process. In the UK the Children Who Wait study was the first to highlight the problem of children drifting in care because of a lack of proper planning for their futures, and it called into question the ability of the care system to parent children (Rowe and Lambert 1973).

Further impetus came from a series of studies summarised in an influential government overview in the mid-1980s, which reported that discharge, or remaining in care, often occurred by happenstance and was not usually the result of social work planning (Department of Health and Social Security 1985). Several of the studies included found that far less attention was given to what was to happen to children after admission than to the decision whether or not to admit, and that if children remained long in care social work attention faded. Children generally returned home as a result of direct action by their parents or because foster parents said they wanted the placement to end. Children's return home was rarely planned and often occurred without the social workers' involvement or prior knowledge. Although social workers were generally opposed to children **entering** care, they rarely worked towards children **leaving** it (Fisher, Marsh and Phillips 1986; Millham and others 1986). The study In and Out of Care found that discharge usually resulted from pressure from the family rather than as a consequence of planned intervention by social workers, who often took a neutral stance towards discharge. Families often took matters into their own hands and social workers were therefore presented with a *fait accompli*, with reunion taking place without their active involvement (Fisher, Marsh and Phillips 1986).

Similarly, a study of social work decision-making reported that there was little evidence of social work activity directed towards exit from care, little evidence of direct work with children or parents and little attention paid to maintaining contact with parents, even where workers expected children to return home. The effects of social workers' 'neutral' stance went unrecognised, but this was in fact creating obstacles to return. They concluded that 'the risk of children remaining in care for lengthy periods is to a large extent created by the manner in which their care careers are managed within social services departments' (Vernon and Fruin 1986: 149).

The Trials and Tribulations study grouped children into those who had entered for reasons of protection (mainly younger children placed for reasons of abuse or neglect) or disaffection (mainly older children placed as a result of their own behaviour) (Farmer and Parker 1991). Rehabilitation had been planned for only 50 per cent of the 'protected' and 34 per cent of the 'disaffected' children who eventually went home. Some returned because placements broke down, or staff or parents pressed for a return, or where planning lost momentum and in the absence of clear intentions from social workers, parents or children stepped in and insisted on return. Few returns resulted directly from a change in the family situation and only 13 per cent of the 'disaffected' returned home after a change in their behaviour.

This study reported a lack of clarity about what needed to happen for the child to be reunified. Sometimes decisions were taken that children should return mainly because they had been in care for a long time, even though nothing had changed. In relation to the 'disaffected', there was a difficult balance of power between social workers, parents and young people, and social workers were often relieved if parents agreed to have their children home. Many of these young people had been admitted for being 'beyond parental control' and took matters into their own hands by running away from care and returning home.

English studies of social work with older children and adolescents during the 1990s indicated that return may occur as a result of the young people's own decisions, even where there had been no change in the behaviour that led to their placement or in family relationships (Bullock, Little and Millham 1993; Sinclair, Garnett and Berridge 1995). A study of older children in residential care also found that by six-month follow-up 43 per cent were not where their social workers had expected them to be by this stage and that events often seemed to be out of the control of either the young person or the social worker (Sinclair and Gibbs 1998). More recently, a study of children in foster care found that the return of children to their families was often poorly planned and supported and often occurred as a result of a series of placement breakdowns, which suggests that little may have changed since these issues were first highlighted in the early 1970s (Sinclair and others 2005). Researchers in the USA have also found that reunion is often unplanned (McMurtry and Lie 1992).

The importance of purposeful case planning

Several studies have argued that purposeful case planning is a key ingredient in the reunification of children. In the USA, two of the experimental studies of specialist reunification schemes reported that focused case planning was an important means to achieving reunification. The Alameda Project concluded that social workers need to take an active role in planning for children's future as soon as they enter care. They must delineate options for the future and facilitate early decision-making. This project used written contracts to agree clear goals with parents (Stein and Gambrill 1977). The authors concluded that the focus on purposeful case planning was the key difference which distinguished the specialist service from the less successful usual service. The FRS study also found that the involvement of parents in joint planning and the setting of objectives was a vital ingredient of the project (Walton and others 1993).

Aldgate's qualitative analysis of the rehabilitation of children in care led her too to conclude that purposeful social work activity was the most influential factor. Social work support, help with problem-solving and emotional difficulties, and practical help with transport all had an effect on return from care (Aldgate 1980). The authors of *Trials and Tribulations* also argued that purposeful planning was important, but acknowledged that it was unclear whether planning itself increased the chances of success or whether social workers only felt confident to plan for those children whose return was most likely to occur, and to be successful. They reported that even when return was planned, this did not necessarily lead to a mobilisation of support or resources for family.

Both Cleaver and Harwin also highlighted the importance of purposeful case planning in the process of return. Cleaver also emphasised the importance of involving both parent and child in planning for return and undertaking direct work with them in furtherance of the goal of rehabilitation (Cleaver 2000). Harwin and her colleagues' study of 100 children entering statutory care, of whom only ten returned home within two years, offers some interesting insights into social work decision-making on reunion (Harwin and others 2001). When social workers initially applied to the courts for care orders they were unsure how family relationships would develop over time and had no immediate aims for rehabilitation. Their decisions in relation to this goal were based on an assessment as to whether the degree of risk could be controlled and that parents could be worked with. Considerations that influenced their decision-making included their sympathy for the mother, respect for children's attachments, perceptions that children were able to seek help when required and faith in the ability of a care order to generate change. Planning the return of children was particularly difficult in cases where mothers misused drugs or alcohol, as in these cases parenting was often positive in other respects.

Service intensity

A comparison of a specialist reunification service with usual services found that the families of children who returned home received more intensive services on average (2.59 hours service per week vs 2.07 hours) (Rzepnicki, Schuerman and Johnson 1997). In contrast, another comparison of specialist and usual services found that service intensity was not associated with outcome, but the authors were at this point referring to a variety of outcomes, not just reunification (Stein and Gambrill 1977). This is consistent with broader studies of family preservation services in the USA, which have not found a direct relationship between service intensity and placement prevention.

Two recent English studies found that once children are reunited with their families, follow-up support is often patchy (Sinclair and others 2005; Ward and others 2004). For example, Ward and her colleagues found that only a quarter of the children had contact with a social worker after their return home. For others, contact with a social worker often centred on practical issues and rapidly tailed off.

Kinship versus non-relative care

The evidence on the effects of placement type on rates of reunification is mixed, and almost all of it comes from the USA. A number of longitudinal studies using large samples, in most cases drawn from agency databases, have found that those placed in kinship care are less likely to return home, or may return more slowly than those in non-relative placements (Courtney and Wong 1996; Courtney 1994; Courtney,

Piliavin and Wright 1997; Goerge 1990; Harris and Courtney 2003; Kortenkamp, Geen and Stagner 2004; Webster and others 2005; Wells and Guo 1999). One study of children reunified within one year of placement found that those in kinship placements went home six times slower (Davis, Landsverk and Newton 1997). A recent English study also found that slightly more children returned home from non-related foster placements (28 per cent) than from placements with relatives or friends (21 per cent) (Farmer and Moyers 2005).

One US study found no difference in reunification rates between those in kinship and those in non-relative placements. However, only children placed for five months or more were included, so this sample was skewed in favour of long-stay children and this may have had an impact upon the findings (Landsverk and others 1996).

It is unclear why children in kinship placements tend to remain longer in care. It is possible that reunification is viewed as less urgent by agencies because children are placed with kin, or alternatively that there is something different about the characteristics or circumstances of children in the two types of placement. For example, at least two studies have found that a higher proportion of children in kinship placements have been removed for neglect, and as we saw earlier children placed as a result of neglect typically remain longer in care (Grogan-Kaylor 2001; Landsverk and others 1996). Also, as we saw in the earlier discussion of child characteristics, in the USA children placed in kinship care are more likely to be African-American, and these children are more likely to come from lone parent families and to experience poverty. There may be an interaction between these factors that leads black children in kinship placements to remain longer in care.

Summary points

- Since concerns about 'drift in care' were first raised in the 1970s, researchers in the UK have consistently reported that children's return home is often unplanned, as little social work attention is given to reunion. Reunification may occur as a result of the actions of parents or children or because placements have broken down.
- There may be little clarity about what needs to change in order for children to return home, and decisions about return may occur irrespective of the presence of any changes in the circumstances that led to placement.
- Several studies have highlighted the importance of purposeful case planning in bringing about reunion.

- Two recent English studies have found that the availability of follow-up support to families once children return home is often patchy, and when it is provided it is usually available only for a short period.
- Most US studies have found that children placed in kinship care tend to be reunited with their families at a slower rate. There is some evidence that this may be because children placed with relatives may have entered care for different reasons or may be more likely to come from lone parent families and experience poverty.

6. The effectiveness of specialist reunification services

This chapter considers the evidence on the effectiveness of specialist reunification services, which have attempted to increase both the likelihood that children will be reunited with their families and the speed with which this takes place. Because randomised controlled trials provide the most robust evidence on the effectiveness of services, the four studies that randomly allocated children either to the specialist reunification service or the 'service as usual' offered by local social work services will be considered separately, followed by a review of the other studies of specialist services of this kind.

Randomised controlled trials

Only four randomised experimental studies of specialist reunification services have been completed, all of them in the USA. All four compared outcomes for those using specialist reunification services with those for children using routine services. Three of these, the Alameda Project, the FRS project and the Preventive Services Demonstration Project (PSDP), found that those using intensive, specialist services were more likely to return to parents, but the fourth, the Charleston Collaborative Project (CCP), found the specialist service to be no more effective than routine services either in returning children home or in improving psychosocial outcomes for children and parents.

- The Alameda study found that 38 per cent of the experimental group returned to their biological parents compared to 27 per cent of the control group (Stein and Gambrill 1979, 1977).
- The New York State PSDP found that 62 per cent of project children, compared to 43 per cent of the control group, had returned to parents or other relatives within six months (Jones, Neuman and Shyne 1976).
- In the FRS study 93 per cent of the FRS group had returned to their parents by the end of the 90-day intensive service period, compared to 28 per cent of the

control group, and 12 months after the service ended 75 per cent of the experimental group (vs 49 per cent of control group) were at home (Fraser and others 1996; Lewis, Walton and Fraser 1995; Walton and others 1993).

- In contrast, at the time the CCP intervention ended (after 90 days), this project proved to be **less** successful at returning children home to their parents (21 per cent) than the routine services (26 per cent), and three months later there were no significant differences between the two groups (Swenson and others 2000).

Although the FRS study showed a higher rate of return for those receiving the specialist service, six months after the service ended the effect was less marked, as 30 per cent of the FRS children had returned to care (some only briefly) while additional control group children had returned home. Fifteen months after the service had started, more of the FRS group had returned to care than the 'routine services' group (21 per cent vs 17 per cent of control group).

At six-year follow-up, the FRS group were found to have had more days at home over this period, but when the number of additional referrals and total involvement by public agencies after initial case closure were compared the two groups were described as generally indistinguishable (Walton 1998). At long-term follow-up (five years) the PSDP also found that no significant difference between the groups remained in terms of the proportion reunited with their families (Jones 1985). The Alameda Project found that just one child in each group had returned to care within a two-year period, so the effectiveness of the project was maintained over this period (Stein and Gambrill 1979). It is perhaps unreasonable to expect, however, that the effects of short-term interventions should persist five or six years later and it is probably more realistic to judge these services by their effects in the medium-term. Rates of reunification and re-entry are summarised in Table 6.1.

The proportion of children who returned home clearly varied dramatically across these specialist projects. As Table 6.1 demonstrates, it is difficult to make clear comparisons between these studies or to draw general conclusions from them. Not only did the nature of the interventions themselves differ, but so did their definitions of reunification (return to parents or to a wider kinship group) and their follow-up periods. The differences in results might therefore be attributed not only to possible 'real' differences in the effectiveness of the services studied but also to the different samples and methods used. All of the children referred to the CCP study were in protective custody as a result of neglect or abuse, as were virtually all of the Alameda Project children. These might be considered a higher-risk group for long-term placement than those in the FRS study, of whom 28 per cent were placed as a result of concerns about child behaviour. It was precisely these older children with behavioural problems that the FRS was particularly successful in returning home

Table 6.1: Reunion and re-entry rates for specialist services (randomised control studies (RCTs) only)

Study	Treatment duration	90* days		6* months		9* months		15* months		<2 years	
Experimental (E) or Control (C) group		*E*	*C* (%)	*E*	*C* (%)	*E*	*C* (%)	*E*	*C* (%)	*E*	*C* (%)
ALAMEDA	*Not specified*										
Returned to parent										38	27
Re-entered										2	2
FRS	90 days										
Returned to parent		93	28			70	42	75	49		
Re-entered								21	17		
PSDP	8.5 months										
Returned to parent or relative				62	43						
Re-entered	*Not reported*										
CCP	90 days										
Returned to parent		21	26								
Returned to parent or relative		52	61	51	59						
Re-entered	*Not reported*										

* From commencement of treatment.

(although this group was also the highest risk group for re-entry to care). Furthermore, the FRS project only worked with children for whom a plan for return home had already been made, who may well have been those for whom reunification was thought most likely to succeed, whereas the Alameda Project and the CCP service recruited children for whom no case plan had yet been made. The latter groups were clearly more likely to include some children for whom a return home was unlikely to be possible.

Another problem is that, unlike the other FRS and CCP, the Alameda Project did not specify a follow-up period, instead following up children during a variable period of up to two years. Also, many children (135) were lost to follow-up because their cases were closed before completion of case plans, but there was no attempt in the analysis to control for the effects of this sample attrition on the results. As for the PSDP, it is important to note that the definition of reunification used in this study encompassed children who returned to other relatives as well as those returning to parents, and this may help to account for the high rate of return. Finally, it has to be borne in mind that the FRS study was conducted in the state of Utah and that, in consequence, two-thirds of the sample came from the Mormon community. As this is such a particular and unusual community, questions arise as to how far the findings of this study are generalisable to other settings.

Bearing in mind these caveats with regard to interpreting the results of these studies, the crucial questions are: what did these specialist services offer and which features of these services were associated with their success? Children referred to the Alameda Project were offered an intensive service using behavioural methods of intervention. It was characterised by purposeful case planning, including the clear specification of goals and treatment and the use of written contracts. Frustratingly, this study gives few other details of the intervention and no information as to how the 'usual services' differed, apart from the fact that the workers delivering these services had slightly higher caseloads. The New York State PSDP provided intensive services by workers with caseloads of only ten, who worked with families for an average of 8.5 months. Services were provided to children aged 14 years or under within six months of placement.

The FRS project was based on the Homebuilders model of intensive family preservation services and drew on attachment theory and social learning theory. It offered intensive casework services for approximately 90 days, with the aim of returning the child home after 15 days. Services were home-based and offered a strengths-focused, partnership-based approach that addressed directly the issues that might lead to re-entry. The model included encouragement of visiting and referral to supportive services, for example counselling or drug treatment. Key features were the setting of goals in collaboration with parents, most commonly in relation to parenting skills, anger management, problem-solving, conflict resolution, communication skills and improving school performance or attendance, plus collaboration with other agencies. Intensive follow-up support was provided after the child's return for the remainder of the 90-day intervention period, during which time ongoing formal and informal supports were set in place. Staff had much-reduced caseloads (6 vs 22 for routine services). Again, few details of the 'routine services' are given, apart from the fact that they were less intensive and employed less experienced, less well-educated staff.

The CCP was a collaboration between four agencies to create a coordinated service for children entering care. It offered families multidisciplinary assessment and case planning which were both more comprehensive and more rapid than the equivalent provided by routine services. If the goal was to return the child home, an inter-agency plan was constructed specifying clear treatment goals. This rapid assessment was followed by a 90-day, intensive, family-based intervention, delivered by the same team (unlike routine services, where assessment and service delivery were undertaken by different teams). However, routine assessment services also appeared to be fairly comprehensive and rapid, although somewhat less so than the specialist service. Indeed, the difference between the two types of service may not have been all that large, as the CCP service that was actually delivered was much less intensive than originally intended, the result of problems with implementation. Also, no details are given as to the nature of the 90-day service that followed the CCP assessment and case-planning phase.

It appears that the common element of all four of these specialist services was the intensity of the service, with low caseloads allowing workers more frequent contact with families than routine services could offer. However, the Alameda Project found that treatment intensity was not predictive of a child's return home (the other studies did not explore this issue). It did find however that among parents in the experimental group, those who agreed to sign written contracts were more likely to be reunited with their children: the predictability of reunification in terms of whether or not a contract was signed was 57 per cent. This suggests that parental motivation and willingness to engage with workers were perhaps important ingredients of success. Other common features were purposeful case planning and the specification and agreement of clear goals with families.

Why, then, were the Alameda and FRS projects apparently more effective than routine services while the CCP service was not? The Alameda Project found that successful rehabilitation was more likely to occur where families had received interventions that resolved the problems leading up to the children's original entry to care. Similarly, the FRS study found that, for those returning home and remaining there, a group of goal-achievement measures for parents and children were associated with success: goals included improved parenting skills, communication skills, anger management skills, school performance and compliance with house rules. Although we know that these two projects used behavioural interventions as part of their repertoire, the studies provide little evidence as to which elements of the service contributed to the differences in rates of return.

It is possible that the CCP service was simply less effective than the other two projects, perhaps because its principal focus was on assessment and case planning rather than on the subsequent implementation of these case plans, or perhaps because plans were made too rapidly after placement. However it is also possible, as Swenson and colleagues suggest, that the CCP study failed to detect an effect because implementation problems meant that the differences between the CCP service and routine services were not very great. The authors also pose the question of whether the 90-day intensive intervention period was simply too short, an issue that has been raised in relation to intensive family preservation services in general (Besharov 1994). However the FRS service was equally brief yet more successful in returning children home.

An important issue that arises from the FRS study is that, although this project was spectacularly successful in returning a high proportion of children to their parents (93 per cent within 90 days), significantly more of the FRS group returned to care compared to those who received routine services. Older children (usually with behavioural problems) were more likely to be returned home by the intensive service than by the routine service, but this was also the group most likely to re-enter care. These older children with child-related causes of placement could probably be returned home with less risk of maltreatment – but paradoxically it was possibly these child characteristics that contributed to the instability of some reunifications. Thus, while the intensive service returned children home rapidly, for some this return was perhaps precipitate and hence unstable. This also raises questions as to whether return was in the best interests of all of these children and whether the longer term child outcomes, in terms of developmental progress or re-abuse as opposed to the service outcomes embodied in these reunification rates, were also positive. The authors of the FRS study hypothesise that these children may have returned to care because the FRS gave insufficient support to help families remain together. They conclude that not all families benefit equally from brief reunification services, but that such schemes may nevertheless help to reunify some children who would not otherwise have been reunified. These issues will recur in the discussion of other studies that follows.

All of the studies reported service outcomes in terms of rates of reunification and two of them reported on re-entry to care, but the CCP study was the only one to report comprehensive findings on child or family-level outcomes. It found that those receiving the specialist service were no more likely than the 'routine services' group to show improvement in terms of psychosocial outcomes for children or parenting stress. Scores for children's problem behaviour showed improvement for children receiving either type of service. The Alameda Project found that the resolution of parent–child interaction problems and of parents' own problems was more likely for those receiving the intensive service (79 per cent vs 49 per cent). Clearly, findings on service outcomes are only one part of the story. In order to judge how successful interventions are, it is important to know whether return is indeed the optimal outcome for each child, but most of these studies did not provide data on psychosocial and family outcomes, or on re-abuse and neglect following reunion that would allow us to judge this.

Other studies of specialist reunification services

Four other comparative studies of specialist reunification services were also undertaken but without random assignment, one of which (Pierce and Geremia 1999) did not report on the effectiveness of the project in returning children home and will not be discussed further at this point. We can be less confident about the relative effectiveness of specialist and routine services reported in these studies as children were not randomly allocated to each group, and thus we cannot assume that they were equivalent in key respects.

Lahti reported on a study of 492 children, comparing a specialist reunification project in Oregon that offered intensive casework to under-12 year olds in care for one or more years to routine services for a similar group of children. She found that children referred to the specialist project were not significantly more likely to return home than those receiving the usual service, with 26 per cent of the children in the project group returning home, compared to 24 per cent in the control group (Lahti 1982). Equally, at 15-month follow-up there was still no significant difference in the stability of placements at home for those who returned,

However, the fact that the intensive project appeared to be no more effective at successfully returning children home than the routine services may, to some extent, be because the children in the two groups were not strictly comparable. The children referred to the specialist project were selected by workers and included only those who fitted the remit of the project, namely children who were thought to have little chance of return home and who were considered adoptable, whereas the comparison group was presumably a more diverse group that included some children considered more likely to return. Although initial prospects for reunification appeared to be dim for the project children, once a return plan had been made parents were generally positive and were generally committed once they were reunited with their children.

More recently, Rzepnicki and her colleagues compared the FRS in Illinois to the routine services available (Rzepnicki, Schuerman and Johnson 1997). The specialist service was similar to the other family preservation services available in that state, in that it was time-limited (6 months) and intensive, its workers had small caseloads, were available to families seven days a week and were assisted by aides. A mix of practical, parent-training, counselling, and substance abuse services were offered to parents. Only children who were relatively new to the child welfare system were eligible for this specialist service (defined as those for whom no more than three reports of maltreatment had been made, from families where at least one child under 13 years had been in placement for less than six months). However, the authors note that the service was plagued by targeting problems occurring as a result of inappropriate referrals.

Outcome data on 1,772 children from 886 families (taken from the agency's database) revealed that, despite the intended six-month time limit, only 54 per cent of the team's cases were closed within this period. However, less cases in the 'routine services' sample were closed during the same time span (although figures for this group are not given). When children in their first placement were compared, it emerged that children receiving routine services were more likely to return home within three months of placement, but after three months the probability that children receiving the specialist service would return increased and surpassed that for the comparison group, eventually exceeding their rate by 20 per cent. In other words, the intensive programme was more effective than the routine services, with 0–12 year olds in placement for more than three months, perhaps because this service undertook planned work with families for a minimum of three months before reunifying them. Children receiving the specialist service had shorter stays in placement and were no more likely to re-enter placement than those receiving routine services.

The Family-Centred Out of Home Care (FCOHC) pilot project was an intensive service that aimed to involve families in planning for their child's return as soon as they entered placement. Workers with small caseloads worked in close collaboration both with families and with other agencies and regularly reviewed progress with families (Lewandowski and Pierce 2002). This study compared 220 children using the intensive service established in certain counties of Missouri to 154 in comparison counties where only routine services were available. The children using the FCOCH service were older, with an average age of 10.7 years compared to 7.7 years for the comparison group, but the groups did not differ significantly in terms of reasons for placement, worker-identified barriers to return or other characteristics. Data from the agency database and case files indicated that, while 42 per cent of the children returned home within 12 months, there were no statistically significant differences between the two groups. There **was** a difference between the groups in respect of re-entry, but not in the desired direction, because the children referred to the specialist project were two-and-a-half times **more** likely to re-enter placement during the 18-month study period than those using routine services. However, among children placed for more than seven days, those referred to the intensive service remained in placement for less days on average (228) than those receiving the routine services (273).

There has also been one study of a specialist reunification service with a single-group design. This study of the Casey Family Services demonstration project provides a helpful description of the nature of the specialist service provided by a private child welfare agency, but gives no details of data collection methods, making it hard to assess the reliability and validity of the data (Fein and Staff 1993). This specialist reunification project offered an intensive service delivered by a two-person team working alongside the state social worker. Reunification was intended to take place after six months, with worker involvement continuing for up to 18 months thereafter. The project was targeted at those children for whom the chances of return appeared slim. For the majority, the principal reason for placement was neglect (79 per cent), while for the remainder the main reason was abuse. Families were offered a 'last chance' service that, if unsuccessful, was be followed by planning for an alternative route to permanence. The service offered training in parental skills, homemaking and budgeting skills, mental health counselling, respite care, transport and support for substance abuse treatment. Its focus was on client strengths and clear goal-setting.

This intensive service targeted at families with multiple and serious problems and returned 38 per cent of the children home, but one-tenth of these returned to care within the two year study period. Over half (56 per cent) did not return home at all, as the intervention led workers to conclude that return was not in the child's best interests and an alternative permanency plan was made (usually after 6–12 months' service). However, as this study had no comparison group of children, it is not possible to judge the effectiveness of the service, as we do not know what might have happened in the absence of the service.

Summary points

The four experimental studies and three other controlled studies discussed here compared outcomes for children referred to specialist reunification services in the USA to those for others receiving routine services. Taken together, the evidence from these seven studies is inconclusive.

- Four studies found that specialist reunification services were more effective than 'routine services' in returning children home – the Alameda, Family First and FRS studies and the PSDP (although the Family First study did not randomly allocate children to its groups, so their equivalence cannot be assumed).
- Three other studies found that specialist reunification services were no more effective than routine services (CCP and FCOCH projects; Lahti 1982). Only the

CCP study was experimental, so the equivalence of children in both groups cannot be assumed in the other two studies.

- Reunification rates for children served by specialist projects ranged from 21 to 93 per cent.

- The wide variation in reunification rates may be the result, in part, of variations in the populations targeted by the different projects and hence in the study samples.

- Features of the successful projects were intensity of services, purposeful case planning, goal-setting with parents and, in some cases, the use of behavioural interventions and/or contracts. However, there was little evidence as to which features of the service, or combination of features, were associated with their effectiveness, other than the Alameda Project's finding that parents who signed written contracts were more likely to have their children returned home.

- Two of the studies that compared rates of re-entry to care found that those who received specialist reunification services were more likely to re-enter care than those receiving routine services (Lewandowski and Pierce 2002; Walton and others 1993). This raises the question of whether efforts to increase reunification might sometimes lead to children being returned home inappropriately, or too soon. However, the Family First and Alameda studies and Lahti's study found no difference in re-entry rates between specialist and routine services.

7.   Re-entry to care

The question of re-entry to care following reunion is an important one. We need to consider not only whether children return to their families but whether they stay there. It is also important to consider re-entry in relation to the rapidity with which children return home. We know that children are more likely to return home in the early months after placement than at a later stage, but what is the likelihood that they will then successfully remain at home after either shorter or longer periods in care? Finally, we need to know which child-, family- and service-related factors are most common among those who are reunited with their families but later return to care.

A key question when considering the research evidence must be: re-entry after how long? Yet this is a particularly difficult question to answer, because different studies have different follow-up periods, making it difficult to compare results across studies. To compound the difficulty, some studies follow up children over varying periods of time. Also, comparison becomes meaningless when it is between studies with very different samples, comparing, for example, rates of re-entry for abused infants with those for a sample of all ages who were admitted for a variety of reasons. Equally, the data available on the factors associated with re-entry depends on the nature of the questions investigated by different studies.

Re-entry in the UK

There is little evidence on rates of re-entry in the UK and much of the evidence available refers to samples of children looked after during the 1980s, when the profile of looked after children was somewhat different. A survey of placement patterns during the mid-1980s found that 18 per cent of those who returned home were re-admitted within the two-year study period, 7 per cent of them twice (Rowe, Hundleby and Garnett 1989). The Going Home study found that 28 per cent of

those discharged within six months had returned to care within one year and that some children who returned 'oscillated' repeatedly in and out of care. Adolescents were a particularly vulnerable group in this respect (Bullock, Little and Millham 1993). This team's later study observed a tendency for oscillation between home and care to replace a single longer stay (Bullock, Gooch and Little 1998). Breakdown rates for children looked after under statutory arrangements and placed 'home on trial' were found to be even higher, as 38 per cent of the mainly younger 'protected' group and 50 per cent of the mainly older 'disaffected' group returned to care (Farmer and Parker 1991).

A more recent study, which focused on children admitted under voluntary arrangements, again found a very high rate of re-entry. Within two years of separation 52 per cent had returned home but then returned to care again and 24 per cent had experienced more than one reunion (Packman and Hall 1998). The most recent British evidence comes from a study of a sample of new entrants to care, of whom 15 per cent of the 133 children discharged home returned to care within two years (Dickens and others, forthcoming) and from a study of a cross-sectional sample of children in foster care, of whom 37 per cent of the 162 children who returned home re-entered care within three years (Sinclair and others 2005). Early findings from an ongoing study of 110 children who were reunified with parents indicate that 54 per cent of these reunions had broken down within two years. Over half of those whose reunion had failed were later returned home again. Of these, 38 per cent were 'oscillators', with two or more failed returns within this period (Farmer and Sturgess 2005). No clear pattern emerges, perhaps because of differences between the samples of children (new entrants/only children whose duration of care was longer on average/admitted under voluntary arrangements only or both voluntary and statutory arrangements). The relatively small sample sizes involved also make it difficult to extrapolate these rates to the wider population of looked after children.

Re-entry in the USA

In the USA early studies of children who had been in care for a minimum of one month found that just under one-third of those who returned home had re-entered care (Fein and others 1983; Wulczyn and others 1980). Later studies of large samples of children drawn from agency databases found that between one-fifth and one-quarter of children reunited with their families subsequently re-entered care. Wulczyn tracked over 83,000 children moving in and out of care in New York State.

He found that 22 per cent of those discharged during a two-year period had re-entered care within four to five years (Wulczyn 1991), a slightly higher rate than the 19 per cent who re-entered during three years in Courtney's study of nearly 7,000 children (Courtney 1995). Festinger found that, in a sample of 210 children placed for a minimum of 60 days prior to discharge 14 per cent re-entered care within one year and just under 20 per cent within two years (Festinger 1996). A later study of 2,616 discharged children found that 24 per cent had re-entered care within two years of re-unification (Wells and Guo 1999). Thus, evidence from the 1990s suggests that, in the United States, around 19–24 per cent of children return to care within two to three years of discharge.

Re-entry rates have generally been a little higher for children referred to specialist reunification services but these studies had much smaller samples, making it harder to generalise from them, and some served families thought to be particularly difficult to reunify. Among a sample composed entirely of abused and neglected children who were given a 'last chance' at reunification 27 per cent of those who returned home re-entered care within 18 months (Fein and Staff 1993). Rates were similar for children referred to two other specialist services, with 28 per cent (Lewandowski and Pierce 2002) and 24 per cent (Rzepnicki, Schuerman and Johnson 1997) of children re-entering care within 18 months. Another study of a specialist scheme found that 30 per cent of children reunited with their families within a 90-day service period returned to care in the subsequent six months (Walton and others 1993).

The risk of re-entry after short periods in care

We saw earlier that children are most likely to be reunified with their families in the early weeks and months after entry to care and that thereafter the probability of reunion declines. However, those children who return home rapidly after placement seem to be at high risk of re-entry to care. The most convincing evidence comes from US studies with very large administrative samples of children, which indicate that the longer a child remains in care before going home, the less likely it is that the child will re-enter (Courtney, Piliavin and Wright 1997; Wulczyn 1991; Wulczyn and others 1980). Both of Wulczyn's studies found the highest rate of re-entry among children discharged to their families within 90 days of entry to care, the latter finding that over one-third of this group subsequently re-entered care.

Similarly, Courtney found that children in care for 90 days or less had higher re-entry rates than others. However, the rate of re-entry varied over time (Courtney 1995).

The likelihood of re-entry declined rapidly over course of the first year following reunion, becoming fairly stable and quite low after two years. Over half of the children who would re-enter care within three years had already done so within eight months.

This pattern of re-entry to care following early reunion may to some extent be the result of a lack of follow-up support. Jones (1998) analysed the correlates of successful reunification for a sample of children aged under 13 years who had been reunified with their parents, of whom 14 per cent returned to care within nine months, and found that those who entered care short-term, returned early and did not receive follow-up support were the most likely to return to care.

Factors associated with re-entry to care

Child-related factors

There is some evidence that children of (approximately) primary school age are more likely to return to care than older or younger children (Bullock, Gooch and Little 1998; Festinger 1996; Rowe, Hundleby and Garnett 1989; Wulczyn 1991), although one study found that infants were significantly more likely to re-enter than those aged 7–12 years (Courtney 1995). One study with a sample of over 2,000 children drawn from an agency database found that for every increasing year of age, the rate of re-entry increased by 10 per cent. Over half of this sample were under four years old, which suggests that, again, it was children in middle childhood who were most at risk of re-entry. However, it is also not uncommon for adolescents to 'oscillate' in and out of care (Bullock, Little and Millham 1993; Packman and Hall 1998).

There is also some evidence from US studies that black children are more likely to re-enter care than white children (Courtney 1994, 1995; Jones 1998; Wells and Guo 1999), although this has been disputed (Courtney, Piliavin and Wright 1997). Other studies have also found that children with learning disabilities (Jones 1998) or health problems (Courtney 1995) are more likely to re-enter than those without such difficulties. There is also evidence that problems in child behaviour may contribute to failed reunion (Fein and others 1983; Fraser and others 1996; Jones 1998; Lewandowski and Pierce 2002). In particular, one study found that children who re-entered care were more likely to have a tendency to violence and self-harm (Packman and Hall 1998: data reanalysed by Bullock, Gooch and Little 1998).

Parent-related factors

There has also been some exploration of the relationship between parental problems and the breakdown of reunion. Researchers have suggested that social isolation and lack of social support (Festinger 1996; Terling 1999), mental health problems (Hess, Folaron and Jefferson 1992; Packman and Hall 1998) or simply the number and/or severity of parental problems (Festinger 1996; Hess, Folaron and Jefferson 1992; Jones 1998; Turner 1984) may be key issues in relation to re-entry. Others have indicated that family poverty is associated with the likelihood of re-entry to care (Courtney 1994; Courtney 1995; Fein and Staff 1993). The issue of parental substance abuse has also been highlighted. Studies from both the UK and the USA have found that children who re-enter care are more likely to have parents with substance abuse problems (Jones 1998; Packman and Hall 1998: data re-analysed by Bullock, Gooch and Little 1998; Terling 1999). One review of the circumstances of 62 children who had returned to care found that 69 per cent of them had parents with substance abuse problems (Hess, Folaron and Jefferson 1992), while another study of a random sample of 88 infants who returned to care found that all but one of them had a parent who reported substance-abuse problems (Frame, Berrick and Brodowski 2000). Poor parenting skills among parents under stress have also been highlighted as an important factor in precipitating re-entry to care (Festinger 1996; Lewandowski and Pierce 2002; Pierce and Geremia 1999; Terling 1999).

Service-related factors

There is some evidence from the USA that placement type may be related to the risk of re-entry. Three US studies have found that children placed in kinship care placements which, as we saw earlier, tend to be of longer duration, are less likely to return to care following reunification (Courtney 1995; Courtney, Piliavin and Wright 1997; Wells and Guo 1999). Wells and Guo found that children whose last placement was non-relative care re-entered 226 per cent faster than those in kinship care.

Courtney and his colleagues have highlighted the fact that a particular problem with studies of re-entry is that they have selected samples of children on the basis of outcome (namely, re-entry). However, these children may have attributes unmeasured by the research which make them in some way different from those with a different outcome (remaining in care), which are not accounted for in the analysis (Courtney, Piliavin and Wright 1997). In an analysis of an agency database containing information on over 20,000 children in California, they used statistical methods to investigate this problem. Consistent with earlier studies, they found that those with short stays in care or multiple placement moves had a higher probability of re-entry, whereas those whose last placement was in kinship care did not. However, once they had corrected for selection bias, African-American children and infants (under one year old at placement) were no longer found to be at higher risk of re-entry than white children or older children. The impact of child health problems on re-entry was also weaker than hitherto thought.

In respect of ethnic origin, Courtney and colleagues hypothesise that, because in the USA African-American parents of children in care have been found more likely to be substance abusers than white parents, and because many black children there enter care as a result of parental substance abuse, it is possible that these children re-enter care as a result of possible continued parental substance abuse. Thus, it is not demographic characteristics such as a child's ethnic origin in itself that makes them vulnerable to re-entry but other social factors commonly associated with these characteristics. The authors suggest that the effects of age and ethnic origin on re-entry to care are complex and that these effects are mediated by other, unidentified factors.

An in-depth review of 62 cases, in which children in the USA were reunited and then later returned to care, raises issues that have some resonance in the UK. It highlighted problems arising from a shortage of social workers, the resulting failure to allocate cases and an associated lack of agency of social work time for contact with families, as well as poor social work assessment (Hess, Folaron and Jefferson 1992). Social work plans were poorly implemented, for example abusers were sometimes allowed continued contact with children despite court orders to the contrary or children were returned where parents did not comply with substance abuse treatments. Even where parents did comply with requirements, for example through attending parenting classes, this did not always result in behavioural change. There was widespread over-optimism about the degree of parental change and an assumption that reunification was best for children. Both this study and others found that children were returned home without sufficient resolution of the family problems that had led to their placement and consequently re-entered care (Fraser and others 1996; Turner 1984)

Is re-entry always a problem?

Just as reunification with their families is generally viewed as a positive outcome for children, re-entry to care is almost invariably viewed as a poor outcome. Certainly, the instability that results from repeated admissions to care may be harmful to children. Re-entry to care may reflect an absence of adequate follow-up services, which might have supported the child in the community. Repeated admissions may also be evidence of failures in assessment, with proper planning for permanent placement repeatedly deferred. For example, a recent English study of children in foster placements found that repeated efforts were some times made to return children home, even when this was not in their best interests. Once they returned, the children rarely received further social work intervention (Sinclair and others 2005). However, some children from families with chronic and severe difficulties may benefit from occasional brief admissions at times of crisis as part of a longer-term plan for family support.

If rates of re-entry are high, the basic assumptions of permanency planning, namely that children can be successfully returned to their families, are called into question. On the other hand, if re-entry rates are low this may suggest that permanency within their families of origin is indeed an achievable goal for many children. The time frame under consideration is also important. Re-entry within a few months of placement may be evidence of service failure, but re-entry some years later should not be viewed in the same way. In order to assess whether re-entry is positive or a negative, more needs to be known about the well-being of children who return home. Equally, there is little available evidence on the link between the nature, intensity and duration of services and patterns of re-entry to care following reunion.

Summary points

- Only a small number of studies in the UK have followed up children reunited with their families. Most of these have found high rates of re-entry to care. There is wide variation in the rates of re-entry identified because of the small sample sizes of these studies and the different ways in which their samples were drawn. Some children were found to have returned home and then re-entered care at least twice within a two-year period.
- Evidence from US studies which tracked large samples of children drawn from agency databases during the 1990s indicates that 19–24 per cent of children in the USA return to care within two to three years of discharge.
- Some US studies have suggested that children in middle childhood are most at risk of re-entry to care, while English studies have identified the phenomenon of adolescents who 'oscillate' in and out of the care system.

■ Several studies have indicated that family poverty, parental drug abuse, the severity of parental problems and poor parenting skills may be associated with a higher risk that reunion might break down. A few other studies have cited parental mental health problems, social isolation and a lack of social support as factors associated with re-entry to care.

■ An in-depth study of re-entry to care in the USA suggested that re-entry was often related to a shortage of social workers and a consequent failure to allocate cases, poor assessment and the poor implementation of case plans, and decisions to return children home in the absence of any change in parental problems or parenting skills.

8. Outcomes for children who return home

Re-abuse

Evidence from both the UK and the USA indicates that children who return home may suffer re-abuse or neglect. A recent three-year follow-up of 596 English children in foster care found that children who were returned home were significantly more likely to be abused than those who were not returned (Sinclair and others 2005). There was strong evidence of re-abuse for 11 per cent of those reunified with their families and some evidence in a further 31 per cent of cases. Another recent English study followed 131 children for 18–48 months after care proceedings were undertaken as a result of abuse or neglect. One-quarter of these children were removed but later returned to live with their parents (Hunt and Macleod 1999). The researchers classified placements at home as either 'safe' or 'risky' and found, surprisingly, that the 'safe' placements were more likely to break down than those placements thought to be risky. In three cases social workers were unable to control the child's contact with an adult male considered a risk, and in two cases a previously non-abusive parent assaulted the child. Most of the breakdowns in 'risky' placements at home resulted from the continuation of severe neglect.

Earlier UK studies during the 1980s and 1990s of children in care had raised similar concerns. In the Trials and Tribulations study one-quarter of the 'protected' group, originally admitted as a result of abuse or neglect, were re-abused or neglected once they returned home (Farmer and Parker 1991). Two-thirds of the children admitted as a result of physical abuse were returned to a parent who had abused them. The nature of the risks was complicated, because almost one-fifth of children placed as a result of the abuse of a sibling were themselves abused once they returned home. A small English qualitative study also found that a number of children re-entered as a result of physical or emotional abuse or because marital difficulties between parents placed them at risk (Thoburn 1980).

For children who have been abused or neglected prior to placement, reunification may therefore be a risky strategy. Three studies by paediatricians in the UK indicate that reunion may be particularly risky for very young children. In Liverpool, Hensey and colleagues followed up 50 children with a mean age of three years who had been placed in care as a result of physical abuse, and of whom half were subsequently returned home. Once home, the children received intensive professional support and intervention from many agencies; nonetheless one-fifth of them suffered re-abuse. The authors of the study considered it an unsatisfactory outcome if any one of the following four characteristics was present in the children: abnormal physical or neurological development, for example failure to thrive; symptoms of persistent emotional disturbance; poor educational progress; or further non-accidental injury following initial abuse. Using this measure of adverse outcome, they reported that those for whom all family contacts were severed fared significantly better than those who were returned home. Less than a quarter of those who returned home had a satisfactory outcome using this measure, compared to over two-thirds of those who remained in foster care. Hensey and colleagues concluded that, in cases where children suffered adverse outcomes, either 'the decision to allow the child home was wrong, or, having allowed the child home, further intervention and supervision was inadequate' (Hensey, Williams and Rosenbloom 1983: 610).

Another study followed up a cohort of 95 abused children in Sheffield, who had a mean age of just under two years, and assessed catch-up growth in terms of height and weight (King and Taitz 1985). Most children either remained at home (64) or were rehabilitated following a short period in foster care (11); 20 were fostered long-term or adopted. At presentation, low scores for height and weight indicated failure to thrive for all children, with no significant differences between the three groups. Over half of those taken into long-term foster care or adopted showed significant increases in height and weight. Significantly fewer of those who remained at home showed an increase in height (11 per cent) or weight (22 per cent), but children fostered short-term and then reunited with their families showed little catch-up growth on either index. The worst scores were therefore observed among those taken into short-term care and then returned home. More recently, a Welsh study followed up a cohort of 49 babies, aged under one, who returned home after placement for three years. Fifteen of them (31 per cent) were re-abused or suffered neglect during this period. Twelve were returned home again after the subsequent abuse and three of these were re-abused yet again (Ellaway and others 2004).

Studies in the USA have raised similar concerns. Terling's analysis of the case files of 59 abused or neglected children reunited with their families revealed that four had been repeatedly and severely physically or sexually abused after their return and twice as many had experienced further neglect; one-fifth re-entered care for these reasons (Terling 1999). Jones analysed outcomes for 445 reunified children, mean age just over four years. She too found that reunited children who were re-referred were twice as likely to have suffered neglect (20 per cent) than physical abuse (9 per cent) (Jones 1998). A descriptive study of 62 children in the USA reported higher figures for re-abuse and neglect, but this was because it focused solely on those who returned to care. It found that neglect contributed to re-entry in 81 per cent of cases, physical abuse also in 81 per cent and sexual abuse in 52 per cent (Hess, Folaron and Jefferson 1992).

The most comprehensive findings on this issue come from Fuller's case-control study in the USA, in which 82 children for whom there were substantiated reports of maltreatment within 60 days of returning home were compared to 92 children for whom no such reports were made during this period (Fuller 2005). Children under 12 years old were more likely to experience re-abuse than older children, with those under one year at the greatest risk. Children who experienced high placement instability and who, we might surmise, may be more likely to be those with significant emotional and behavioural problems, were eleven times more likely to be maltreated upon their return. Children returned to caregivers suffering from mental illness were nine times more likely to be re-abused, and re-abuse was also eight times more likely for those who had been in care for three years or more and five times more likely for those returned together with siblings to a lone parent. These findings suggest that uncertainty and stress for parents (and children) may trigger re-abuse, indicating that follow-up support is likely to be needed to ensure a safe transition to the home environment.

Psychosocial outcomes

Evidence from both English and US studies suggests that children reunited with their families are likely to experience worse psychosocial outcomes than those who remain in long-term care or are adopted. Quinton and Rutter (1988) compared scores for psychosocial functioning for girls in residential care aged 7 to 13 years with their scores 14 years later. Those who had returned to homes with pervasive quarrelling and disharmony were significantly more likely to have poor outcomes in early adulthood on a validated measure of social functioning (Rutter B scale) than those who remained in care. This suggests that the emotional climate of the families to which children were returned was not a factor that influenced decisions to rehabilitate them, and indeed Thoburn (1980) found that the families of children who returned home were no more stable emotionally than those of children who remained in care.

A six-year follow-up of a cohort of 149 children in the USA also used standardised measures (Achenbach's Child Behaviour Checklist, the Youth Self-Report and the Adolescent Risk Behaviour Survey) to compare emotional and behavioural outcomes for 63 young people who were reunified with their families with those for 86 who remained in care. It found significantly more emotional problems, self-harming behaviour, substance misuse, risk behaviours and total behavioural problems among those who were reunified than among those who were not (Taussig, Clyman and Landsverk 2001).

In the study of foster care by Sinclair and his colleagues, rejection following reunion was associated with deteriorating mental health among children. Children aged 11 and over who returned home from placements in foster care were found to have emotional and behavioural problems as serious as those of children entering residential care, including running away, self-harm, substance abuse and aggression (Sinclair and others 2005). These problems were significantly less common among children in long-term foster care or adoptive homes. The researchers composed a composite outcome rating on the basis of social worker and carer ratings of emotional and behavioural problems that revealed, overall, being at home was associated with worse emotional and behavioural outcomes.

Lahti (1982) similarly devised a general well-being measure constructed from ratings of health, adjustment at home, at school and in social situations, to compare outcomes for 492 children reunified, adopted or remaining in foster care. Using this measure, reunified children were found to have experienced less well-being and less stability by follow-up 15–24 months later. Child well-being scores were higher where placements were seen as permanent by parents or carers, and Lahti famously observed that 'Perception of permanence was the key' (1982: 568).

Children reunified with their families have been found to experience worse problems at school than those remaining in care. In the 2005 study by Sinclair and colleagues, a measure of educational adjustment, which comprised measures of educational performance and participation, showed no improvement for children who returned home, in contrast to those who those remained in care or were adopted. Similarly, Taussig and colleagues found that 21 per cent of the reunified children in their cohort dropped out of school, compared to only 9 per cent of those who remained in care (Taussig, Clyman and Landsverk 2001). The Trials and Tribulations study also found that educational outcomes were poor for children who returned home. For 57 per cent of the older, 'disaffected' children who were reunited with their families, school attendance was poor or non-existent, although no comparisons with others remaining in care were made.

The same study reported that, for those who had originally been admitted to care for offending, the re-offending rate after they returned home was 70 per cent. Taussig and colleagues found that reunited young people were significantly more likely to have been arrested (49 per cent) than those who remained in care (30 per cent), as did Sinclair and his colleagues. Minty's 25–30-year follow-up of 100 children previously in care, who were matched with 100 disadvantaged children from the same local area but who had not previously been in care, came to similar conclusions (Minty 1987). He reported that young men discharged home or to relatives by the age of 15 years were significantly more likely to have adult convictions than those who stayed in foster care after the age of 15, although the former group were also more likely to have had convictions as juveniles, which may help to explain this finding.

Overall it is clear that, although only a few studies have assessed the risk of re-abuse or analysed emotional and behavioural outcomes, there is sufficient evidence to raise concern about outcomes for children reunited with their families. These studies raise questions about the quality of assessment, intervention and follow-up for children and families and more research is needed into the risks and outcomes associated with reunification.

Summary points

- The small number of studies of looked after children in the UK that have investigated the outcomes for children reunited with their families have indicated that some may be at considerable risk of re-abuse or neglect.
- Three UK studies by paediatricians have shown that very young children reunited with their parents following placement as a result of abuse are at high risk of re-abuse and continued neglect.
- Studies in the USA have raised similar concerns and have also found that children were more likely to re-enter care as a result of further neglect than as a result of re-abuse. One study also found that infants were at the highest risk of re-abuse compared to older children.
- A comprehensive US study of re-entry to care as a result of re-abuse found that children who had been in care for three or more years and those returned to caregivers who suffered from mental illness were more likely to suffer re-abuse. Those who had experienced a high degree of placement instability, and who were

likely to be those with the most severe emotional and behavioural problems, were also at high risk of further maltreatment.

- Evidence from both English and US studies suggests that children reunited with their families are likely to experience worse psychosocial outcomes than those who remain looked after or are adopted. Those who return home have been found to have more serious emotional and behavioural problems, poorer social functioning, educational participation and adjustment, and higher rates of re-offending than those who continue to be looked after.

- Although few studies have examined outcomes for children reunited with their families, the findings of those that have done so raise questions about the quality of social work assessment, decision-making and follow-up in respect of children who return home.

9. Implications for policy, practice and research

Although there have been a small number of notable studies in the UK, much of the evidence on reunification comes from the USA and it is unclear how far these findings are transferable to the British context. Research findings on the timing of reunion and on the child, family and service characteristics associated with reunion have been similar in many respects on both sides of the Atlantic, but the relationships between the probability of reunion and ethnic origin or placement in kinship care have yet to be explored in the UK. While studies in both the UK and the USA have focused on patterns of return and re-entry to care, in the UK more attention has been given to in-depth explorations of the process of return. However, there has been less attention in either country to child-level outcomes, for example the welfare and developmental outcomes for children reunited with their families.

It is clear that most children who enter care return home quite quickly. Concern about reunification centres on those children who remain looked after for longer periods. The fact that most children who do return home tend to do so after only a few weeks or months may be related to the reasons they have entered care, or their parents' attitudes and behaviour, or to a range of other factors that have been outlined here. It has long been clear from the research that rapid decision-making and purposeful planning on the part of social workers is vital if children are not to drift through a series of placements. Studies have suggested that social workers may promote reunion by engaging parents in joint planning and supporting them in maintaining contact with their children. Such approaches may indeed assist the process of reunion, but other issues, for example the quality of parent–child relationships, may also be influential.

However, the fact that, overall, children are more likely to go home shortly after placement than later on, together with the common assumption that reunification is necessarily the best outcome for children, has sometimes led to over-hasty attempts to return them home. This tendency is reinforced by pressure to contain the considerable costs of caring for separated children. Yet, and as we have seen, reunification may take place without adequate assessment and children may be reunited with their families when this is not in their best interests. Rapid re-entry to care and poor psychosocial outcomes may signal a failure to meet children's needs, and the few studies that have examined re-abuse and neglect following reunion have also raised worrying concerns. For children with a history of abuse and neglect, particularly those who are very young, there is evidence that reunification may be a risky strategy, one that must be accompanied by adequate assessment and follow-up support.

Implications for policy and practice

In the UK relatively little attention has been given to the issue of reuniting looked after children with their families compared to the attention given to the question of placement. A sharper focus on this issue would be timely, given the trend in recent years for children to remain in care for longer and the fact that adoption is likely to be a route to permanence for only a tiny minority of looked after children. However, care is needed to ensure that the focus is on achieving positive outcomes for individual children, measured in terms of child well-being, and not solely on service outcomes, measured in terms of rates of discharge. Equally, reunion needs to be considered as part of a continuum of services for children, and efforts to achieve it, where appropriate, should be properly resourced.

A focus on improving service outcomes by returning more children home, or returning them home more rapidly, cannot in itself ensure positive outcomes for the individuals involved. In any case, as research both in England and the USA has shown, rates of discharge are related to wider issues of policy and practice, such as local thresholds for entry to care (Dickens and others, forthcoming; Wulczyn 1991). Some local authorities may readily accommodate children while others may offer this service only to those experiencing the highest levels of need. These strategies reflect differing views on the use of placement, with some using placement as a form of short-term support for families in crisis and others using it only as a last resort. Not surprisingly, because the group of children accommodated by agencies with lower thresholds for placement is likely to include a proportion of those with less severe difficulties, a higher proportion will return home more rapidly than those under authorities with high thresholds for looking after children. Other system factors, such as the availability of foster and residential placements or alternative family support services, and the financial resources to pay for these, may also influence rates of placement and discharge (Biehal 2005). Comparing rates of return across authorities can tell us little about the effectiveness of different policy and practice approaches to both the use of placement and the rehabilitation of looked after children in meeting children's needs.

The preoccupation with administrative categories such as rates of placement and rates of discharge derives not only from understandable agency concerns with containing costs but also from the assumption that placement is 'bad' and discharge is 'good'. Yet, a focus on achieving desirable service outcomes, such as lower rates of placement and higher rates of discharge, is unlikely to be the best way of ensuring positive outcomes for individual children. This is particularly important given the trend for younger children to enter care as a result of abuse or neglect and to remain there longer as a result of the seriousness of their difficulties (Department of Health 2001). It is therefore essential to address two related questions. First we must ask 'for which children, in which circumstances, is a return home likely to be beneficial?'; second, we must consider which types of service are needed to promote this reunion.

This approach obliges us to consider the care system as one element within a broader continuum of service provision, ranging from family support at one end, through the use of placement for some children, to purposeful social work activity to ensure permanence and then on to follow-up support. A flexible view of service provision is needed, including a willingness to tailor a varied range of services to meet individual children's needs, and a prioritisation of attention to child outcomes over service outcomes. For those children for whom a return to their families is considered the best outcome, focused planning for reunion is essential. This is just as important as planning for the care of those who remain looked after, which is usually given more attention. Equally, follow-up support may be needed once children return home. Yet research has indicated that this is rarely provided, despite the fact that there may have been little change in the problems that led to placement and that readjustment to family life may be difficult when family membership has changed during the child's absence, as is often the case. Planning and support are needed therefore to ensure not only that children are reunited with their families, when this is thought to be in their best interests, but also that they and their families receive follow-up services for an adequate period of time after reunion takes place.

Because not all children may be safely reunited with their families, a broader conceptualisation of what constitutes reunification may also be more helpful than more extreme commitments to returning children to their families, as Maluccio and his colleagues have suggested. It may be more helpful to view reunification as a continuum ranging from full re-entry into the family to occasional contact to maintain the child's sense of connectedness and involvement with their family of origin (Ainsworth and Maluccio 1998; Maluccio, Abramczyk and Thomlison 1996; Maluccio, Pine and Warsh 1994).

Implications for research

Apart from some important English studies of reunion, in general the lack of policy attention to this issue in the UK is mirrored by a paucity of research on the topic. The pervasive belief that reunion with their families is good for most children has rarely been tested. Children may be discharged before child and family problems have been sufficiently ameliorated, or may be returned to neglectful or dangerous environments in the belief that rapid discharge is desirable. Few studies in either Britain or the USA have investigated the health, developmental, psychosocial and behavioural outcomes for children reunited with their families and compared them to those for similar children who remain in care. It is important to consider how these outcomes are related to the age at which children are first looked after, the reasons for which they enter care and the prior psychosocial functioning of children and parents. Prospective studies are likely to be more helpful here than those that identify groups of children on the basis of specific outcomes, such as re-entry to care. Studies of this kind can ensure that those who experience the outcome of interest can be compared to those who do not, making it easier to tease out the variables that may predict this outcome.

It would also be helpful to know more about the views of the children themselves of return and to understand more about the difficulties some have in resolving complicated feelings about identity, belonging and family loyalty when deciding on the nature and level of contact they wish to have with their families. Although reunion with families is likely to be the best means of achieving permanency for many children and for ensuring that they have a 'family for life', more research is needed to identify the circumstances in which a return home is both safe and desirable.

Appendix 1: Review protocol

The research questions for this review and the criteria on which studies were selected have been set out in the Introduction.

This review cannot be considered a true systematic review, although it has adopted some of the core principles and procedures used in systematic reviews. The research questions it addresses are broader than those typically addressed by systematic reviews registered with the Campbell Collaboration, which in most cases focus on the effectiveness of particular interventions. It is common for reviews of effectiveness to focus only on a small group of studies, usually randomised controlled trials, although other designs may also be acceptable. Because this review addresses a broader set of research questions, it includes a much broader range of studies than would be typical for a systematic review. However, consistent with the procedure for systematic reviews, only studies that meet explicit criteria for relevance and study quality are included.

Study design

The review critically evaluates studies that employ a wider range of methodologies than is normally found in systematic reviews. Systematic reviews of medical research normally set up a hierarchy of evidence, with randomised control trials (RCTs) as the 'gold standard', followed by quasi-experimental studies, cohort studies and so on, with descriptive studies at the lowest level of the hierarchy. However, this view of the methods likely to generate sound evidence has been criticised as being narrow and rigid and questions have been raised as to the transferability of this model from a medical context to a social policy context (Dixon-Woods, Fitzpatrick and Roberts 2001). One problem with adopting the (medical) hierarchy of evidence in a review of research on children's services is that it is difficult to carry out experimental studies with randomised controls in this service context and practitioners are reluctant to cooperate with such studies, for ethical reasons. Furthermore, in the UK researchers on social care have shown a preference for qualitative methodologies, with quantitative and experimental approaches typically being viewed with hostility (Fisher 2002). Accordingly, experimental studies of social work have been rare in the UK, meaning that if the Cochrane guidelines were employed in the review, most UK studies would automatically be excluded. Data from studies that could offer valuable information to policy-makers and practitioners would be lost to the review if their designs were considered less robust within the terms of a framework developed for reviews of medical interventions.

Assessment of what constitutes the 'best' evidence should not, therefore, be based on a hierarchy that gives precedence to experimental designs, as non-experimental studies may provide important data not only on the effects of interventions, but also on process and other factors which may help to explain why interventions have particular effects (Rychetnik and others 2002). Although it is harder to draw conclusions on effectiveness from studies with non-experimental designs, these may nevertheless be useful in answering different types of research questions, providing important insights into outcomes for children and their correlates and into the ways in which interventions come to be associated with particular types of change. For these reasons, non-experimental studies (both quantitative and qualitative) will also be included in the review. Studies included in the review will be classified according to the taxonomy of sufficient study design developed by Baldwin and colleagues (2002), as shown in Appendix 1 (Baldwin and others 2002) .

There is a danger of underestimating the value of evidence if the research methods used are 'lower' in the hierarchy, because studies that are modest methodologically may nevertheless offer important findings (Baldwin and others 2002). Studies with non-experimental designs may provide important insights into how interventions operate and how they come to be associated with particular types of change. In their account of realistic evaluation, Pawson and Tilley (1997) argue that the proper role of researchers is to develop theories of change, which try to explain how, why and in what circumstances interventions produce change. A similar theories of change model has been used to evaluate community initiatives in the USA (Connell and Kubisch 1998). Such theory-driven models may be particularly appropriate to the constantly shifting service context of social work, because experimental models are difficult to implement in these conditions both for practical reasons and because they are often viewed as unethical by practitioners (although it might be countered that it less ethical to provide services to children **without** rigorously testing whether they are effective). While theory-driven approaches do not normally figure in the 'hierarchies of evidence' they are beginning to be used in studies of social work.

Although experimental studies may provide evidence as to whether a particular effect has occurred, they may not adequately explain what has brought about the observed effect and the conditions and contexts in which it is likely to occur. However, qualitative studies can often shed light on these issues. This has been accepted even within the field of medical research, for example Black has observed that RCTs 'provide information on the value of an intervention shorn of all context, such as patients' beliefs and wishes and clinicians' attitudes and beliefs, despite the fact that such variables may be crucial to determining the success of the intervention' (Black 1996; Petticrew 2001). There are a number of models of the role of qualitative research. For example, Popay and Williams (1998) outline the 'enhancement' model, in which qualitative methods can help to explain why interventions may or may not work, and the 'difference' model in which qualitative research explores 'taken for granted' behaviour, perceptions or cultures.

The Campbell Collaboration has acknowledged that process evaluations using qualitative or mixed methods may provide the best means of answering certain types of research questions, providing evidence on issues such as the ways in which professional or service-user behaviour can help or hinder the implementation of services (Popay and Dunston 2001). Qualitative studies may not only complement findings from experimental studies, making an important contribution to the total body of evidence. They may also compensate for the failure of experimental studies to take account of the process of an intervention and of the impact both of its context and of the attitudes and beliefs of practitioners and service users upon outcomes.

Quality appraisal

The inclusion of non-experimental studies in a research review does not mean that the quality of these studies should be disregarded. The risk here would be that policy and practice might come to be influenced by misleading findings from poor quality studies. In any case, experimental studies themselves may be of variable quality. The degree of credence we give to findings from any study, regardless of whether it is experimental or non-experimental, should derive from a clear assessment of the quality of its design, implementation, analysis and the way conclusions are drawn. Recognising that experimental methods are not the only means of producing useful knowledge and that experimental studies have been rare in social care (in the UK, at least), the Social Care Institute for Excellence (SCIE) suggests that a more subtle and inclusive approach is needed to the assessment of the quality of social care knowledge rather than a hierarchy of evidence that prioritises experimental approaches (Fisher 2002).

Appraising qualitative studies

While there are widely accepted standards in respect of the scientific rigour and credibility of studies using quantitative methods, which are assessed in terms of the reliability and validity of the measures used, their use of systematic data collection, attention to any confounding variables and objectivity, no current consensus exists as to the criteria by which qualitative research should be judged. This issue has been hotly debated, with positions ranging from a rejection of the need for any quality criteria at one extreme to a retention of concepts common to quantitative and qualitative research at the other (Spencer and others 2003).

There are no standardised instruments in qualitative research, thus validity cannot be seen as inherent in a particular instrument that could be tested in some way. As a result, concerns about the validity of methods have often been translated into concerns about the rigour with which research is conducted. There is fairly widespread support for the idea that all qualitative studies should be conducted in a rigorous and transparent manner so that others can judge their methodological validity. There is more controversy, however, about whether or not validity in terms of credibility or truth claims can be judged, reflecting the wide range of philosophical positions underpinning different approaches to qualitative inquiry. Views range from a belief that qualitative research knowledge can be a 'true' representation of an objective reality to the opinion that no single 'truth' exists and therefore no single understanding can be privileged over alternative understandings (Spencer and others 2003).

The concept of reliability has also sparked much debate among qualitative researchers regarding the possibility, or desirability, of establishing whether another researcher analysing the same issue or the same data would arrive at the same conclusions. Among those who regard reliability as a relevant issue for qualitative researchers, some have recommended that clarity is needed over the conduct of data analysis while others have argued that reliability can be enhanced through the use of more than one researcher to code and analyse data.

Finally, there is no consensus on the possibility of generalising from qualitative studies, because unlike quantitative data, their data cannot be tested for statistical significance. One approach is that there are no context-free meanings because evaluation is intrinsically context-specific. However, a more common position is that generalisation about the wider applicability of findings is both desirable and possible (Mason 1996; Silverman 2000). Although there are inevitably a range of approaches to generalisation within qualitative inquiry, there appears to be fairly widespread agreement that some discussion of the wider relevance, or limitations in scope, of a study is an important aspect of quality (Spencer and others 2003).

The above discussion indicates the difficulty in devising a simple set of criteria by which the quality of studies might be appraised. Reviewing these debates, several commentators have cautioned against the use of checklists of criteria for judging qualitative studies (Baldwin and others 2002; Dixon-Woods, Fitzpatrick and Roberts 2001; Spencer and others 2003). Researchers' claims that purposive sampling, triangulation, grounded theory and so on that have been used in a study may not necessarily guarantee that it is of sufficient quality, so an appreciation of the value, limitations and appropriate use of such techniques is essential. Accordingly these commentators have argued that, while every effort must be made to take a systematic approach to quality appraisal, within a framework of clear quality criteria a reviewer must nevertheless exercise their informed professional judgement.

A range of study designs and data collection methodologies will be considered appropriate for inclusion in this review, meaning that clear and transparent appraisal criteria are needed that can be used to assess the quality of studies of different types. A 'bottom-line' of criteria by which all types of studies can be judged would be the most helpful tool for a review of this kind. However, because qualitative research is philosophically distinct from quantitative research and is grounded on very different assumptions, different criteria may be needed for the assessment of its quality (Spencer and others 2003). In this review, studies will be selected for inclusion if they satisfy a set of essential quality criteria appropriate to all types of studies and also criteria specific to either quantitative or qualitative approaches.

Inclusion criteria: study quality

Drawing on a range of literature on the assessment of qualitative work and on the evaluation of quantitative work, Baldwin and colleagues have devised a list of essential and desirable criteria for assessing research quality (Baldwin and others 2002). Their schema will be adopted in this review and studies will be included if they meet the following essential criteria.

- Is the research question clear?
- Is the study design appropriate to answer the question (good face validity)?
- Sampling
  - *Quantitative*: was the sample size adequate for the analysis used and has it been drawn from an appropriate population
  - *Qualitative*: is the sample adequate to explore the range of subjects and settings and has it been drawn from an appropriate population?
- *Data collection*: is data collection adequately described and rigorously conducted to ensure confidence in the findings (systematically collected)
- *Data analysis*: is there evidence that the data analysis has been rigorously conducted to ensure confidence in the findings (are analytical procedures explicit)?
- Are the population and the intervention described?

Baldwin and her colleagues argued that their essential criteria were identified as those which have the potential to alter the findings of the research and therefore must be met reasonably well in order to ensure the internal validity of the study and to ensure the findings are sound. While there may be differences in interpretation of the results, if these essential elements are met the findings should remain robust. On the basis of the above quality appraisal criteria, a summary checklist for quality appraisal was designed – see Table A1.3.

Criteria for inclusion in the review

Studies will be included in the review if:

1. They address the review's research questions (as specified in Table A1.1).
2. They are of sufficient study design (as specified in Table A1.2).
3. They meet our quality appraisal criteria (as specified in Table A1.3).

Studies to be excluded:

- Essays and other expressions of expert opinion.
- Grey literature: because a substantial body of peer-reviewed literature on this topic exists, and as a result of time constraints, non-peer-reviewed literature was excluded.
- Studies of care leavers (age 16 and over) who return home on leaving care. The circumstances of these young adults are quite different from those of children who are too young to live independently.
- Studies which are simply historical or legal accounts.

Table A1.1: Study selection criteria for inclusion in the review

	Inclusion criteria	Exclusion criteria
Geographical coverage	Studies that relate to the UK and USA.	Studies that relate to other countries.
Timing of studies	a) Studies of family reunification from 1973 onwards. b) Studies of looked after children in the UK that refer to reunification (undertaken since 1991).	a) Studies published prior to 1973. b) Studies published prior to 1992.
Population of interest	Children under the age of 16 years who return home from care placements.	Care leavers age 16 and over.
Dimensions of studies	Studies that report on outcomes for children, including processes whereby outcomes are achieved.	Historical or legal accounts; studies of staff training, support, etc.
Study design	Studies with experimental or observational designs, using either quantitative, qualitative or mixed methods of data collection (see Table A1:2).	Grey literature, policy or opinion pieces, multiple reports from single study.
Quality appraisal	Studies judged to be of sufficient quality according to the essential quality appraisal criteria for this review (see Table A1:3).	Studies poorly designed and constructed.

Table A1.2: Study design classification

Research Type	Research methodologies				
	Experimental		Observational		Other
Data collection methods	RCTs	Quasi-experimental	Controlled studies (cohort, case control).	Uncontrolled (before and after, cross-sectional, descriptive).	Expert opinion, grey literature, multiple reports.
(1) Quantitative methods (surveys, secondary analysis of large data sets)					
(2) Qualitative methods (in-depth interviews, ethnographic, discourse analysis, participant observation, etc.)					
(3) Mixed methods					
Final review	Included as sufficient study design				Excluded

Note: Adapted from Baldwin and others (2002)

Table A1.3: Summary checklist for quality appraisal

STUDY OVERVIEW		
Endnote ID code		
Bibliographic details	Author, data, title, publication details.	
Purpose	What are the aims of the study?	
Study features	What is the study design code (see study design map)?	
STUDY APPRAISAL	*Qualitative research*	*Quantitative research*
Essential criteria		
Clarity of research question	Is the research question clear?	
Appropriateness of design	Are study design, methodology, data collection methods and outcome measures appropriate?	
Sampling	Is the sample adequate to explore the range of subjects or settings?	Is the sample appropriate and its size adequate for the analysis used?
Data collection	Does the research privilege subjective meaning? Was the data collection explicit?	Is the response rate sufficient and has non-response been analysed?
Data analysis	Was the data analysis explicit?	Were the analysis techniques clear and appropriate?
	Are the findings substantiated by the data? Attrition adequately dealt with?	
Desirable criteria		
Reflexivity	Is consideration given to alternative explanations of the results, and to any limitations of methods or data that may affect results?	
Generalisability	If any claims to generalisability have been made, do these follow logically, theoretically or statistically from the results?	
Evaluative summary	Summary of strengths and weaknesses of study.	
Quality status	A, B, C or D (see Table A1.4).	

Note: Table adapted from Baldwin and others (2002)

- Studies which cover only particular features of family reunification, for example training or support or payment levels for foster carers, but do not report on outcomes for children.

The selection criteria for inclusion in this review are summarised in Table A1.1 (adapted from Baldwin and others 2002).

Table A1.4: Coding of quality status

Category A	Studies that meet the appraisal criteria with no, or very few, flaws.	Included in final review.
Category B	Studies that meet all or most of the appraisal criteria well, with some flaws.	Included in final review, with study concerns noted.
Category C	Studies that include many and/or serious flaws that have the potential to affect the findings.	Excluded from review.
Category D	Studies that present insufficient data on methodology to allow an appraisal of quality.	Excluded from review.

Note: Table adapted from Baldwin and others (2002)

Data extraction

A form was designed for data extraction showing the information to be recorded in different fields on an Access database (see **p.88**).

Data synthesis strategy

Aggregating data from a range of quantitative studies through the use of meta-analysis (using statistical techniques) of raw data would not be appropriate to this review as a result of the wide range of study designs to be included. Instead, a narrative approach will be taken to combine study findings, characteristics and validity. Narrative synthesis can examine effectiveness, discuss similarities and differences and compare outcomes (Boaz, Ashby and Young 2002).

Search strategy

Searches were undertaken in two phases by Julie Glanville and Vickie Orton, Centre for Reviews and Dissemination, University of York:

1   A search on family reunification from 1973 to date.
2   A search on children in the care system from 1991 to date.

The databases and systems searched were as follows:

Database	Interface/Version and supplier
Applied Social Science Index and Abstracts (ASSIA)	CSA Web interface *http://www.csa1.co.uk/*
British Library catalogue	Internet interface *http://www.bl.uk/catalogues/blpc.html*
Caredata	Web interface *http://195.195.162.66/elsc/caredata/caredatasearch.htm*
International Bibliography of the Social Sciences (IBSS)	BIDS WebSPIRS interface *http://www.bids.ac.uk/*
PsycINFO	BIDS WebSPIRS interface *http://www.bids.ac.uk/*
SIGLE (grey literature)	ARC WinSPIRS service Access provided by the University of York
Social Science Citation Index (SSCI)	Web of Science *http://wos.mimas.ac.uk/*
Social Work Abstracts	ERL WebSPIRS *http://web5.silverplatter.com/webspirs/start.ws* CRD subscription
Sociological Abstracts	ARC WinSPIRS service Access provided by the University of York

Search 1: Search on family reunification from 1973 to date

ASSIA

ASSIA was searched (26/02/2003) from its earliest records to 1994 records for family reunification for the period 1986–2003 (07/03/2003). Records obtained numbered 206.

Caredata

Caredata was searched (26/02/2003) for family reunification for the whole date coverage of the database (07/03/2003).

International Bibliography of the Social Sciences

IBSS was searched (26/02/2003) for family reunification for the period 1975–2003.

PsycINFO

PsycINFO was searched (26/2/2003) from its earliest records to 1994 records for family reunification for the period 1872–2003 (07/03/2003). Records obtained numbered 136.

SIGLE

SIGLE was searched (07/03/2003). Records obtained numbered 27.

Sociological Abstracts

Sociological Abstracts was searched (26/02/2003) for family reunification for the period 1986–end of 2002 (07/03/2003). Records obtained numbered 237.

SSCI

SSCI was searched (26/02/2003). Records obtained numbered 575.

Social Work Abstracts

Social Work Abstracts was searched (26/02/2003) for family reunification for the whole date coverage of the database (20/3/03). Records obtained numbered 245.

Search 2: Children in the care system from 1991 to date

ASSIA

ASSIA was searched (11/03/2003). Records obtained numbered 761.

Caredata

Caredata was searched (10/03/2003).

IBSS

IBSS was searched (10/03/2003). Records obtained numbered 147.

PsycINFO

PsychINFO was searched (11/03/2003). Records obtained numbered 825.

SIGLE

SIGLE was searched (11/03/2003). Records obtained numbered 20.

Sociological Abstracts

Sociological Abstracts was searched (06/03/2003). Records obtained numbered 61.

SSCI

SSCI was searched (10/03/2003). Records obtained numbered 500.

Social Work Abstracts

Social Work Abstracts was searched (10/03/2003). Records obtained numbered 209.

Forward searching from bibliographies given in publications was undertaken by Nina Biehal. Internet searches were also carried out for publications subsequent to the search date, up to April 2005. Titles and abstracts were checked and irrelevant records and duplicates deleted, leaving 270 potentially relevant publications for review.

Data extraction form

Endnote ID code	
Bibliographic details	Author, title, place, publisher.
Year of publication	
Main area of enquiry	Note focus of study.
Relevance of study	Has study met inclusion criteria for relevance to research question? 1 = yes; 2 = no; 3 = uncertain.
Study design and quality	
Study design code	A = RCT; B = quasi-experimental study; C = controlled observational study; D = uncontrolled observational study; E = expert opinion and other reports. 1 = quantitative methods; 2 = qualitative methods; 3 = mixed.
Study characteristics	Type of research, data collection instruments, sample source and size, length of any follow-up period, study setting.
Quality overview	A = meets appraisal criteria well with no or very few flaws. B = Meets all or most appraisal criteria well, with some flaws. C = has many flaws that have potential to affect the findings. D = insufficient data on methodology to allow appraisal of quality.
Details of population and intervention	
Age of sample	
Sex and ethnicity	
Reasons in care	
Time looked after	
Nature of intervention	Specialist reunification scheme, normal social work service.
Key features of intervention	Recruitment strategy, theory/methods, duration, follow-up.
Location of study	Country
Context	Any relevant contextual factors, e.g. local authority social work, private or voluntary sector service, demonstration project.

Data extraction form (*cont'd*)

Findings	
Main findings	Brief summary of main findings.
Process	Any factors relating to delivery of intervention that affect its effectiveness, e.g. implementation, acceptability, training, recruitment.
Outcomes (including events, numbers, p-values)	Proportion of children reunified. Proportion of children who re-entered care. Factors associated with success/stability. Factors associated with non-return. Factors associated with breakdown of reunion.
Other notable findings from study	
Comments	

Note: Adapted from Baldwin and others (2002) and Centre for Reviews and Dissemination (2001).

Appendix 2: Study tables

Table A2.1: Studies of specialist reunification services

Author	Specialist interventions (RCTs)	Sample	Sample size	Follow-up	Results
Jones, Neuman and Shyne (1976); Jones (1985) (USA)	*Preventive Services Project* Intensive services provided for a mean of 8.5 months compared to usual services.	Age: 14 or younger; 81% in care; 19% recently discharged.	314 children (from 195 families).	6 months and 5 years.	After 6 months, 62% of project children (vs 43% of control group) had returned to parents or other relatives, but after 5 years no significant differences.
Stein and Gambrill (1977, 1979) (USA)	*The Alameda Project.* Intensive service using behavioural methods compared to routine services. Agreed goals; written contracts.	Age: 0–15 years, in foster placements, for whom no case plan yet made. 58% of the Alameda group (31% of control group) aged 0–6. Most placed for neglect.	293 for outcome analysis.	Variable period: <2 years.	Of the specialist group, 38% returned to parents vs 27% of the control group. Resolution of parental problems and parent–child interaction problems more likely resolved for specialist groups (79% vs 49%).
Swenson and others (2000) (USA)	*Charleston Collaborative Project (CCP)* Brief, intensive, multidisciplinary, rapid assessment, inter-agency case plan. Comparison to routine services.	Age: 0–16 years (mean age, 8 years) and taken into protective custody for abuse or neglect.	72 (from 45 families).	At service completion (90 days) and 3 months later.	CCP no more effective than routine services. At 90 days, 21% CCP (vs 26% control group) reunified. At 6 months, 51% CCP vs 59% control returned (ns). No difference in treatment effects on child behaviour or parenting stress.

Table A2.1: Studies of specialist reunification services *(cont'd)*

Author	Specialist interventions (RCTs)	Sample	Sample size	Follow-up	Results
Walton and others (1993); Lewis, Walton and Fraser (1995); Fraser and others (1996); Walton (1998) (USA)	*Family Reunification Service (FRS)* Intensive, brief (90 days) casework services compared to routine services. Goals agreed with parents. Aim to return child after 15 days plus intensive follow-up for 75 days.	Age: 1–17 years (mean age, 10.8). In care >30 days, for whom reunification was the case plan. Mean no. of prior placements: 2.8; 67% Mormon. Placement reasons: 45% abuse/neglect; 28% child behaviour.	110 (from 47 families).	90 days, then 9 and 15 months after service started. Also 6 years later.	At 90 days, 93% of FRS group returned to parents (vs 28% control group), but 6 months later 30% re-entered care. At 15 months, 70% of FRS group at home (vs 42% control group), but 21% of FRS group had re-entered care (vs 17% of control group).
Author	**Specialist interventions (other controlled studies)**	**Sample**	**Sample size**	**Follow-up**	**Results**
Lahti (1982) (USA)	Cohort study comparing a specialist project (intensive casework) with routine services for children.	Under 12 years old and in care >1 year. Specialist group chosen by staff (those thought adoptable and unlikely to go home).	492	15–24 months.	No significant difference in rate of return (26% project group vs 24% control group). No difference in stability of placements at follow-up. 'Perception of permanence was the key'.
Lewandowski and Pierce (2002) (USA)	*Family-Centred Out of Home Care (FCOHC)* Intensive service compared to routine services. FCOHC involved families in plans for return when child was placed.	FCOHC group: 10.7 years; control group: 7.7. Placements: 60% for neglect or abuse; 10% for behavioural problems.	374	12 months (return) <18 months (re-entry).	Overall, 42% returned home within 12 months but FCOHC children were no more likely to do so than control group. Among those who returned, FCOHC children were 2.6 times more likely to re-enter placement.

Table A2.1: Studies of specialist reunification services (*cont'd*)

Author	Specialist interventions (other controlled studies)	Sample	Sample size	Follow-up	Results
Pierce and Geremia (1999) (USA)	*Family Reunion Service (FR)* Intensive service for 60 days.	FR cohort compared to matched group of children receiving usual services.	312 children from 169 families; mean age, 8.2 years.	16 months after return home.	Successful reunion more likely when parents were motivated to change. FR children less likely to re-enter care after return home.
Rzepnicki, Schuerman and Johnson (1997) (USA)	*Family First* Time-limited, intensive service compared to routine services. Encouraged parental visiting; offered practical support.	Age: 0–12 years (mean age: 5.3 years), in placement <6 months. Placement mostly the result of parental substance abuse or emotional problems; 24% for child behaviour.	Outcome data on 1,772 children (from 886 families).	2 years.	Project children less likely to return home in first 3 months of placement, but probability of return surpassed comparison group after 3 months, eventually exceeding their rate by 20%. Overall, 40% returned in 6 months, 48% within 9 months and 53% within 1 year

Table A2.2: Studies of usual social work service or other interventions

Observational: controlled studies (usual social work service)				
Author	Focus of study	Sample	Follow–up	Key findings
Bullock and others (1993) (UK)	Identified factors that predict likelihood and success of reunion. Case controls.	Followed up samples from three earlier studies: (a) n = 450; (b) n = 104; (c) n = 321. All ages.	Variable: 5 years for sample (a)	Sample (a): most returners in <6 months aged under 12 years and placed as a result of temporary family crisis. Returners between 6 and 24 months mostly adolescents, often with ambivalent parents.
Bullock, Gooch and Little (1998) (UK)	Identified factors that predict likelihood and success of reunion. Those identified in 1987 study tested on prospective sample. Case controls.	All ages: (a) follow-up of samples from 1993 study, n = 875; (b) new sample, n = 463; (c) intensive study, n = 31.	Variable	Sample (b): of those returning after <6 months, 60% not previously separated. Most were placed as a result of parental illness or family crisis, or a temporary rupture between adolescents and parents. Of those placed >6 months, the quality of family relationships was a key predictor for return.
Courtney (1994) (USA)	Longitudinal study of new entrants to care with case controls. Explores effects of child, family and service variables on rate of reunion.	Random sample of 10% drawn from agency database; n = 8,748 (all first-time entrants). All ages, with 45% <4 years when placed; entered care, 1988–91.	<3.5 years	Just under half reunified with parents in <3 years. Most returned immediately after placement. Of those reunified, nearly half were home in <6 months and 70% in <1 year. Those in kinship care returned at a slower rate; 4–12 year olds were fastest. Those placed for sexual abuse reunified faster than those placed for neglect.
Courtney and Wong (1996) (USA)	Longitudinal study with case controls. Explores effects of child, family and service variables on timing of different types of exit from care.	All first-time entrants; n = 8,625. Data drawn from agency database. Entered care Jan–June 1988. Age: 0–16 years.	<4 years	58% reunified with parents, relatives or guardians in <4 years. Probability of return decreases rapidly in first 5 months after reunification. Reunion faster for ages 4–6 and is slower if black, family on benefits, placed for neglect rather than abuse or in kinship care.

Table A2.2: Studies of usual social work service or other interventions (*cont'd*)

Observational: controlled studies (usual social work service)				
Author	Focus of study	Sample	Follow-up	Key findings
Courtney, Piliavin and Wright (1997) (USA)	Longitudinal study with case controls. Re-analysis of effects of child, family and service variables on timing of exit from care.	All abused and neglected first-time entrants to care. Age 12 or under; n = 21,484.	<4 years	Placement instability, kinship care and short stays in care associated with re-entry. Black children and infants proved no more likely to re-enter care than others, and the effect of child health problems was less strong than hitherto found.
Davis and others (1996) (USA)	Descriptive study using case controls to compare outcomes for those reunited/not reunited. Analysis of case files.	865 children aged <12 years, in statutory placements, who had a reunion plan and were in care 72 hours–18 months when plan was made.	1 year after reunion decision made	More likely to be reunited if mother visited at level stipulated by court, child came from two-parent family, entered for sexual abuse and was white.
Fanshel and Shinn (1978) (USA)	Prospective study with case controls.	Stratified random sample of first admissions; n = 624. Included if under 13 years and stayed in care 90 days or longer.	5 years	Multivariate analysis showed contact: (a) associated with reasons for admission and with discharge; (b) had positive and negative effects on behaviour and attainment; and (c) had some effect on probability of discharge.
Fuller (2005) (USA)	Case-control study (data drawn from agency database and case records). Investigated predictors of re-abuse following reunion.	Children with substantiated reports of maltreatment within 60 days of reunion matched with a sample for whom no such reports were made; n = 174.	60 days	Predictors of maltreatment recurrence were: (1) child under 12 years, and especially if under 1 year; (2) mental illness of caregiver; (3) in care ≥3 years; (4) high placement instability; (5) placement in kinship care; and (6) child returned with siblings to a lone parent.

Table A2.2: Studies of usual social work service or other interventions (*cont'd*)

Author	Focus of study	Sample	Follow-up	Key findings
Observational: controlled studies (usual social work service)				
Jones (1998) (USA)	Case-control study comparing children who re-entered care to those who did not (data drawn from agency database and case records).	All children who were reunified with parents; n = 445 (from 245 families). Age: 0–12 years; in care for 72 hours or more.	9 months after reunion	Correlates of re-entry were family poverty, parental drug abuse, an unsafe environment, inadequate housing, the child's problems (medical, school, behavioural, mental health) and child being black.
King and Taitz (1985) (UK)	Prospective cohort study of catch-up growth following abuse.	Children aged 2 months–12 years, either placed in long-term foster care, short-term care or stayed at home; n = 95.	32 months	Children suffering child abuse show greater catch-up growth when taken into long-term foster care compared to those who stayed at home or stayed in care short-term. Worst scores were for those in short-term care.
McMurtry and Lie (1992) (USA)	Longitudinal study with case controls. Compared modes and rates of exit from care for different ethnic groups.	Entered care 1979–84; n = 775. Long-stay sample: sampling strategy meant 97% placed >6 months after start of study.	2–7 years	30% of this long-stay sample returned home; 20% of these returns were unplanned. Black children half as likely to return home as white children in any given time period. Children with disabilities went home at slower rate.
Millham and others (1986) (UK)	Prospective study.	Representative sample of 450 children. All ages.	2 years	Family factors a strong predictor of reunion. Contact associated with early return.
Minty (1987) (UK)	Retrospective study of impact of care history on adult offending.	100 children in care matched with 100 other disadvantaged children.	25–30 years	Those discharged to relatives by age 15 more likely to have convictions as adults than those who stayed in care after age of 15 years.

Table A2.2: Studies of usual social work service or other interventions *(cont'd)*

Observational: controlled studies (usual social work service)				
Author	Focus of study	Sample	Follow-up	Key findings
Quinton and Rutter (1988) (UK)	Psychosocial and parenting outcomes in adulthood comparing girls in residential care with 51 girls never admitted to care.	Sample of 93 girls in care and 51 non-care (81 care and 41 non-care at follow-up). Age: 7–13 years at baseline (21–27 years at follow-up).	14 years	Girls who had returned to disharmonious homes significantly more likely to have poor outcomes in early adulthood on a validated measure of social functioning.
Sinclair and others (2005) (UK)	Case-control study of outcomes for children in foster care.	Sample of 596 children, of whom 162 returned home at some stage.	3 years	Reunified children more likely to be re-abused, have poor educational performance and participation and have emotional and behavioural difficulties at follow-up (self-harm, aggression, substance abuse, offending).
Taussig, Clyman and Landsverk (2001) (USA)	Prospective cohort study comparing those reunified (n = 63) with those who were not (n = 86).	Children aged 7–12 years on admission (13–17 years at follow-up), in care at least 5 months; n = 149.	6 years	Reunified youth had more negative outcomes than those who did not return home in terms of self-destructive behaviour, risk behaviour, criminal convictions, dropping out from school, school attainment, internalising behavioural problems and total behavioural problems.
Turner (1984) (USA)	Retrospective comparison of services and outcomes for children successfully reunited to others who re-entered care.	Random selection of 50 reunited children who remained at home and 50 of those who re-entered care.	Not given	Little help provided while in placement and no follow-up support. Case planning and referral to community services even less likely for group who later re-entered care.

Table A2.2: Studies of usual social work service or other interventions (*cont'd*)

Observational: studies without control groups				
Author	Focus of study	Sample	Follow-up	Key findings
Albers, Reilly and Rittner (1993) (USA)	Factors that predict reunification. Analysis of agency database.	All 404 children age 0–9 years in placement.	3 years	African-American children and those from poorer families reunified slower than white children.
Aldgate (1980) (UK)	Qualitative study of factors associated with reunion.	Interviews with 60 parents plus professionals and foster carers.	–	Purposeful social work activity was key to return. Likelihood of return also related to reasons for entry.
Barth and others (1987) (USA)	Factors associated with reunion of physically abused children. Review of case records (closed cases).	Purposive sample of 208 physically abused children.	–	Less severe abuse, higher socio-economic status and better behaviour at school increased the chance of return.
Benedict, White and Stallings (1987) (USA)	Longitudinal study with stratified random sample. Compared time in care for black and white children.	Children of all ages placed for the first time, for ≥24 hours; n = 689.	<6 years	Median stay was 6 months for both black and white children and 67% of both ethnic groups returned to parents within 6 years.
Cleaver (2000) (UK)	Family contact for children in foster care. Case-file survey plus intensive study. Findings on reunion from the latter.	Intensive study; n = 33. Age: 5–12 years. All placed in >3 months.	Intensive study: 1 year	Contact helpful if purposeful, supported and resourced, if the parent was motivated and the parent–child attachment was strong.
Courtney (1995) (USA)	Factors associated with re-entry to care.	Criterion sample of 6,831 children returned to parents or relatives. Age: 0–16 years.	3 years	More likely to re-enter if aged 7–12 years; black; had health problems; poor; in care for a shorter time; multiple placement moves.

Table A2.2: Studies of usual social work service or other interventions (cont'd)

Observational: studies without control groups				
Author	Focus of study	Sample	Follow-up	Key findings
Davis, Landsverk and Newton (1997) (USA)	Factors associated with reunion. Analysis of case files.	All children under 13 years who entered care and left within 1 year; n = 445.	<9 months after return	Slower return if: learning disability; entered for neglect (especially severe neglect) or physical abuse; lone parent; mother didn't visit; in kinship care.
Dickens and others (forthcoming) (UK)	Patterns of admission and discharge from 24 English local authorities.	New entrants to care. Data drawn from agency databases: n = 5,000; questionnaire sample: n = 251.	2 years	Those leaving care: 27% in <6 months; 53% within 2 years; 15% re-entered care within 2 years. Agencies with higher start rates for admission had a higher turnover and vice versa.
Ellaway and others (2004) (UK)	Follow-up of physically abused babies who were returned home.	Babies under 1 year when abused; n = 49.	3 years after incident	Re-abused or suffered neglect: 15 (31%); returned home after the subsequent abuse: 12; abused again: 3.
Farmer and Parker (1991) (UK)	Exploratory, descriptive, cross-sectional study of children returned 'home on trial'. Explored factors associated with successful return.	All ages; n = 321. All placed ≥2 years. 172 were 'protected' (younger; placed for abuse/neglect) and 149 'disaffected' (older; placed for behaviour/offending).	2–14 years after return home	Only 50% of returns planned, of which 43% broke down. Breakdown often instigated by parent or child. Abused children returned sooner than neglected children. Of the 'protected' group, 25% were re-abused. For the 'disaffected', placement brought few lasting changes in behaviour.
Fein and others (1983) (USA)	Outcomes of different types of permanent placements. Case records and interviews.	187 children reunited/adopted/ in long-term foster care. 84% <12 years.	12–16 months	32% of reunions disrupted. Children in care for neglect reunified slower. Social work support declined sharply after return.

Table A2.2: Studies of usual social work service or other interventions (*cont'd*)

Observational: studies without control groups				
Author	Focus of study	Sample	Follow-up	Key findings
Festinger 1996 (USA)	Re-entry to care following reunion. Data drawn from computer records and questionnaires submitted to social workers.	All reunited children under 10 years; n = 210.	2 years	14% re-entered care within 1 year. Re-entry more likely where a parent had more problems and the child was aged ≥6. Regression analysis showed key factors predicting re-entry: poorer parenting skills; less social support; more unmet service needs.
Finch, Fanshel and Grundy (1986) (USA)	Cross-sectional study of patterns of discharge	Data drawn from agency database: 20,066 children in care, 1974-6. Mean age at entry: 9 years.	None	If placed <1 year, increase of 1 year in care; 40% decrease in probability of return (but not so for long-stay sample). Increase in 5 years of age at entry: 17% decrease in probability of return.
Fisher, Marsh and Phillips (1986) (UK)	Placement and discharge of children. Retrospective qualitative study (interviews and review of case records).	Interview sample: n = 55. Age: ≥8 years. 350 case records reviewed.	–	Reunion rarely planned, usually the result of pressure/action by family. Social workers paid little attention to discharge.
Frame, Berrick and Brodowski (2000) (USA)	Re-entry to care of infants originally placed for abuse. Analysis of computer records plus focus groups comprising parents and professionals.	n = 88 children under 12 months at placement.	4-6 years	Predictors of re-entry: maternal substance abuse was 'a near perfect' predictor; maternal criminal history (drug-related activity including prostitution); child age (re-entry more likely if <1 month at entry); housing problems; number of abuse reports; receipt of post-reunion services. Contact did not predict re-entry.

Table A2.2: Studies of usual social work service or other interventions (cont'd)

Observational: studies without control groups			
Author	Focus of study	Sample	Follow-up	Key findings
George (1990) (USA)	Longitudinal study of factors associated with time in care.	Cohort of first-time entrants to care. Data drawn from agency database: n = 1,196. All ages.	6–8 years	Probability of reunion declined over time for those placed for abuse or neglect, but not for those placed as a result of behavioural problems. Ethnic origin, region and number of placements also associated with time in care.
Glisson, Bailey and Post (2000) (USA)	Longitudinal study of factors associated with time in care.	Cohort of 700 children entering care or youth custody. Age: ≥5 years. Siblings excluded.	3 years	Child emotional and behavioural problems and placement as a result of sexual abuse decreased the probability of reunion. Effects of age and gender mediated through interaction with other variables.
Grogan-Kaylor (2001) (USA)	Comparison of reunification outcomes for those in kinship or non-relative care.	Data drawn from agency database: n = 75,339. All children placed over a 4-year period. Age: 0–13 years.	4 years	Children in kinship care reunified slower, perhaps because they were different to those in non-relative care, were more likely to be black, over 1 year old and placed for neglect.
Harris and Courtney (2003) (USA)	Interaction of ethnic origin and family structure with timing of reunification.	Data drawn from agency database: n = 9,162. Children in first placement in care. All ages.	Variable: <4 years	More black children came from single-parent families: interaction of ethnic origin and family structure meant they stayed longer in care.
Harwin and others (2001) (UK)	Prospective qualitative study of children placed on care orders.	Consecutive sample of 100 children from 57 families, of whom 10 reunited with parents. 76% <10 years.	21 months	No clear plans for reunion when Care Orders made. Decisions on reunion based on a view that risk could be controlled and that parents could be worked with.

Table A2.2: Studies of usual social work service or other interventions (*cont'd*)

Observational: studies without control groups				
Author	Focus of study	Sample	Follow-up	Key findings
Hensey, Williams and Rosenbloom (1983) (UK)	Outcomes for children placed after physical abuse.	50 children admitted to care as a result of abuse. Mean age: 3 years.	<4 years	Reunified children more likely to be re-abused, to have abnormal physical or neurological development, emotional disturbance or poor educational progress.
Hess and Folaron (1991) (USA)	Parental ambivalence and re-entry to care. Retrospective qualitative study comprising interviews with families and professionals plus analysis of case files.	n =40. All ages.	–	Ambivalent parents poorer, often had learning disabilities and lacked social support. Substance-abusing parents not usually ambivalent.
Hess, Folaron and Jefferson (1992) (USA)	Family and service-system factors associated with re-entry. Retrospective qualitative study comprising interviews with families and professionals plus analysis of case files.	n = 62	–	Re-entry often occurred where parents had multiple, serious and chronic problems and where workers were inexperienced and/or over-optimistic and did little direct work.
Hunt and Macleod (1999) (USA)	Outcomes of judicial decisions in child protection cases.	131 children on care orders, 34 of whom were reunified. All ages: 56% <5 years; 80% <10 years.	18–48 months	Some placements at home broke down as a result of abuse, difficulty in controlling the child's contact with an adult male considered a risk, or severe neglect.

Table A2.2: Studies of usual social work service or other interventions (*cont'd*)

Observational: studies without control groups			
Author	Focus of study	Sample	Follow-up	Key findings
Kortenkamp, Geen and Stagner (2004) (USA)	Role of family factors in predicting reunification. Analysis of agency database plus phone interviews.	n = 133. Mean age: 8 years.	<7 years	42% reunited. Children who were older, black or in kinship care were less likely to be reunited.
Landsverk and others (1996) (USA)	Impact of child psychosocial functioning (measured using Achenbach's Child Behaviour Checklist) on probability of reunification.	Cohort of new entrants to care; n = 669. Age: 2–16 years. Children stayed in care for at least 5 months.	18 months	Multivariate analysis showed that those in non-kinship placements were more likely to return if older, placed for sexual or emotional abuse, or removed from two parents. Those with identified emotional/behavioural problems were half as likely to return as those without.
Lu and others (2004) (USA)	Ethnicity and case outcomes. Data drawn from agency records.	n = 3936. Age: 2–16 years. Referred for abuse, neglect or caretaker absence.	17 months	30% reunited. African-Americans less likely to return home than white children.
McCue Horwitz, Simms and Farrington (1994) (USA)	Link between developmental problems experienced by the child and exit from care. Paediatric assessment 7 months after placement.	n = 242. Age 1 month–<8 years. Majority: < 2 years.	7 months	Reunion less likely if developmental problems, older or non-white. 85% of those with all 3 predictors not reunited.
Milner (1987) (USA)	Retrospective study of children recently discharged from care.	Random sample: n = 75. Stratified by time in care (2 months–18 years)	None	Children who spent shorter periods in care were those visited frequently by their parents and for whom the parent–child relationship was positive.

Table A2.2: Studies of usual social work service or other interventions (*cont'd*)

Observational: studies without control groups				
Author	Focus of study	Sample	Follow-up	Key findings
Packman and Hall (1998) (UK)	Voluntary admission to care: support, protection and control.	n = 153 Age: 0–16 years. Many placed as a result of behavioural problems.	2 years	High re-entry rates: 6 months after entry 46% returned home and were still there; 24% had returned but re-entered care. 2 years after entry 52% had gone home and then re-entered care; 24% had >1 reunion.
Rowe and Lambert (1973) (UK)	Cross-sectional, descriptive study of long-stay sample.	n = 2812. All placed for at least 6 months; 75% for 2 years or more. All under 11 years of age.	None	After 6 months in care, chance of reunion home is slim. Most children in need of permanent placements had problems of health, development or behaviour.
Rowe, Hundleby and Garnett (1989) (UK)	Descriptive study of admissions, discharges and placement endings for a cross-sectional sample.	n = 5,688. All ages.	2 years	Conclusions refer to all types of placement endings, including change of placement, not simply to discharge.
Seaberg and Tolley (1986) (USA)	Cross-sectional study of predictors of length of time in care. Data drawn from computerised case records.	n = 3,950. Mean age 11.3 years.	None	Longer stay in care if child is abandoned, older, black, or has physical or learning disability. Shorter stay if placed for abuse, child behaviour, parent–child relationship problems or if parental contact continues.
Sinclair and others (2005) (UK)	Outcomes for children in foster care. Prospective study comprising questionnaires and interviews.	596 children, of whom 162 returned home at some stage (others adopted or in long-term foster care).	3 years	Strong evidence of re-abuse among 11% of children reunited and some evidence of re-abuse for 31%. Reunited children more likely to display difficult behaviour and have educational problems.

Table A2.2: Studies of usual social work service or other interventions (*cont'd*)

Author	Focus of study	Sample	Follow-up	Key findings
Observational: studies without control groups				
Smith (2003) (USA)	Effect of drug use and drug treatment compliance upon reunification. Cross-sectional study: parents interviewed once.	Subset of a probability sample stratified to over-represent parents with drug abuse allegation n = 159 parents (498 children) with at least 1 child under 18 years in care placement.	21–30 months	Children placed as a result of parental drug use allegations returned 2 times faster than those placed for other reasons. If parents completed drug treatment, children returned 6 times faster. Completing treatment in itself increased rate of reunification, irrespective of ongoing drug use.
Terling (1999) (USA)	The correlates of re-entry for abused and neglected children. Follow-up of children on agency database plus study of 59 case files.	n = 1,515	Few weeks–3.5 years	20% re-entered care as a result of abuse or neglect (n = 59). Children were twice as likely to enter for neglect as abuse. A history of previous abuse referrals was associated with re-entry (n = 1,515).
Thoburn (1980) (UK)	Qualitative study of children returned 'home on trial'.	n = 34. All ages.	–	Reunion often unplanned. Influenced by: attitudes of parent, child and social worker; nature of support offered; the placement. Determination of parents was key. Some re-entered as a result of abuse or marital difficulties between parents.
Vernon and Fruin (1986) (UK)	Social work decision-making. Prospective, qualitative study.	n = 185. All ages. Cross-sectional sample of children in care plus cohort of new entrants.	<1 year	One-third reunited; time in care linked to reason for admission. Most left care as a result of actions of family or carers. Lack of social work planning for return. Workers' 'neutral' attitude hindered reunion.

Table A2.2: Studies of usual social work service or other interventions (cont'd)

Observational: studies without control groups				
Author	Focus of study	Sample	Follow-up	Key findings
Webster and others (2005) (USA)	Likelihood of reunification for sibling groups. Data drawn from agency database.	Cohort of 15,517 children who entered care with siblings in 2000 and stayed for ≥5 days.	12 months or at discharge if sooner	Children placed with siblings more likely to reunify than those placed apart, but size of sibling group had no effect. Placement as a result of neglect, placement instability and placement in kinship care all associated with lower likelihood of return home.
Wells and Guo (1999) (USA)	Reunification and re-entry. Data drawn from agency database.	Children not previously placed. Age: 0–15 years; n = 2,616.	2 years	Black infants reunified 60% slower than white infants, but rate of reunion for black children increased with age. Children who were older and black spent only few months in care and if placed in kinship care were more likely to re-enter.
Wulczyn (1991) (USA)	Caseload dynamics and re-entry to care. Data drawn from agency database.	n = 932. All ages.	<5 years	22% re-entered care. Those discharged after brief placement more likely to re-enter. Time in care related to demand on agency foster care resources.

References

Ainsworth, F and Maluccio, AN (1998) 'The policy and practice of family reunification', *Australian Social Work*, 51, 1.

Albers, EC, Reilly, T and Rittner, B (1993) 'Children in foster care: possible factors affecting permanency planning', *Child and Adolescent Social Work Journal*, 10, 4, 329–41.

Aldgate, J 'Identification of factors influencing children's length of stay in care', in Triseliotis, J (ed.) (1980) *New Developments in Foster Care and Adoption*. London: Routledge & Kegan Paul.

Baldwin, S, Wallace, A, Croucher, K, Quilgars, D and Mather, L (2002) *How Effective are Public and Private Safety Nets in Assisting Mortgagors in Unforeseen Financial Difficulties to Avoid Arrears and Repossessions? Review Protocol.* York: Social Policy Research Unit, University of York.

Barth, RP, Snowden, LR, Ten Broek, E, Clancy, T, Jordan, C and Barusch, A (1987) 'Contributors to reunification or permanent out-of-home care for physically abused children', *Journal of Social Service Research*, 9, 2/3, 31–45.

Benedict, MI and White, RB (1991) 'Factors associated with foster care length of stay', *Child Welfare*, 70, 45–58.

Benedict, MI, White, RB and Stallings, R (1987) 'Race and length of stay in foster care', *Social Work Research and Abstracts*, Winter, 23–6.

Berrick, JD, Barth, RP and Needell, B (1994) 'A comparison of kinship foster homes and foster family homes: implications for kinship foster care as family preservation', *Children and Youth Services Review*, 16, 1/2, 33–63.

Berridge, DA and Cleaver, H (1987) *Foster Home Breakdown*. Oxford: Blackwell.

Besharov, D (1994) 'Looking beyond 30, 60 and 90 days', *Children and Youth Services Review*, 16, 1/2, 445–51.

Biehal, N (2005) *Working with Adolescents. Supporting families, preventing breakdown.* London: British Agencies for Adoption and Fostering.

Biehal, N, Clayden, J, Stein, M and Wade, J (1995) *Moving On. Young people and leaving care schemes.* London: HMSO.

Black, N (1996) 'Why we need observational studies to evaluate the effectiveness of health care', *British Medical Journal*, 312, 1539–45.

Boaz, A, Ashby, D and Young, K (2002) *Systematic Reviews: What Have They Got To Offer Evidence-based Policy and Practice? ESRC UK Centre for Evidence Based Policy and Practice: Working Paper 2.* London, Queen Mary College, University of London.

Bowlby, J (1951) *Maternal Care and Mental Health.* Geneva: WHO.

Bullock, R, Gooch, D and Little, M (1998) *Children Going Home. The reunification of families.* Aldershot: Ashgate.

Bullock, R, Little, M and Millham, S (1993) *Going Home. The return of children separated from their families.* Aldershot: Dartmouth.

Centre for Reviews and Dissemination (2001) *Undertaking Systematic Reviews of Research on Effectiveness. CRD's Guidance for those Carrying Out or Commissioning Reviews. Report,* 2nd edn. University of York: Centre for Reviews and Dissemination.

Cleaver, H (2000) *Fostering Family Contact.* London: The Stationery Office.

Connell, J and Kubisch, A 'Applying a theory of change approach to the evaluation of comprehensive, community initiatives: progress, prospects and problems', in Connell, J (ed.) (1998) *New Approaches to Evaluating Comprehensive Community Initiatives,* Vol. 2, *Theory, Measurement and Analysis.* Washington DC: Aspen Institute.

Courtney, M and Wong, YI (1996) 'Comparing the timing of exits from substitute care', *Children and Youth Services Review,* 18, 4/5, 307–34.

Courtney, ME (1994) 'Factors associated with the reunification of foster children with their families', *Social Service Review,* 68, 1, 81–108.

Courtney, ME (1995) 'Reentry to foster care of children returned to their families', *Social Service Review,* 69, 2, 226–41.

Courtney, ME, Piliavin, I and Wright, B (1997) 'Note on research. Transitions from and returns to out of home care, *Social Service Review,* 71, 652–67.

Davis, I, Landsverk, J, Newton, R and Ganger, W (1996) 'Parental visiting and foster care reunification', *Children and Youth Services Review,* 18, 4/5, 363–82.

Davis, IP, Landsverk, J and Newton, RR 'Duration of foster care for children reunified within the first year of care', in Berrick, JD, Barth, RP and Gilbert, N (eds) (1997) *Child Welfare Research Review,* Vol. 2. New York: Columbia University Press.

Department of Health (1991) *Patterns and Outcomes in Child Placement.* London: HMSO.

Department of Health (2000) *The Children Act Report 2000.* London: Department of Health.

Department of Health (2001) *Children Looked After by Local Authorities Year Ending 31 March 2000.* London: Department of Health.

Department of Health and Social Security (1985) *Decision-Making in Child Care. Recent research findings and their implications.* London: HMSO.

DfES (2003) *The Children Act Report 2002*, Nottingham: DfES Publications.

DfES (2004) *Children Looked After in England (Including Adoptions and Care Leavers): 2003–2004*. London: National Statistics/DfES.

DfES (2005) *Children Looked After by Local Authorities Year Ending 31 March 2004*. London: National Statistics/DfES.

Dickens, J, Howell, D, Thoburn, J and Schofield, G (forthcoming) 'Children starting to be looked after by local authorities in England: an analysis of inter-authority variation and case centred decision making', *British Journal of Social Work*.

Dixon-Woods, M, Fitzpatrick, R and Roberts, K (2001) 'Including qualitative research in systematic reviews: opportunities and problems', *Journal of Evaluation in Clinical Practice*, 7, 2, 125–33.

Ellaway, BA, Payne, EH, Rolfe, K, Dunstan, FD, Kemp, AM, Butler, I and Sibert, JR (2004) 'Are abused babies protected from further abuse?' *Archive of Diseases of Childhood*, 89, 845–6.

Fanshel, D and Shinn, E (1978) *Children in Foster Care: A longitudinal investigation*. New York: Columbia University Press.

Farmer, E and Moyers, S (2005) *Children Placed with Relatives and Friends. Placement patterns and outcomes. Report to the DfES*. Bristol: University of Bristol.

Farmer, E and Parker, R (1991) *Trials and Tribulations*. Norwich: The Stationery Office.

Farmer, E and Sturgess, W (2005) Personal communication. Bristol: University of Bristol.

Fein, E, Maluccio, A, Hamilton, V and Ward, D (1983) 'After foster care: outcomes of permanency planning for children', *Child Welfare*, 62, 6, 485–562.

Fein, E and Staff, I (1993) 'Last best chance: findings from a reunification services program', *Child Welfare*, 72, 1, 25–40.

Festinger, T (1996) 'Going home and returning to foster care', *Children and Youth Services Review*, 18, 4/5, 383–402.

Finch, S, Fanshel, D and Grundy, J (1986) 'Factors associated with the discharge of children from foster care', *Social Work Research and Abstracts*, 22, 1, 10–18.

Fisher, M (2002) 'The Social Care Institute for Excellence: the role of a national institute in developing knowledge and practice in social care', *Social Work and Social Sciences Review*, 10, 1, 36–64.

Fisher, M, Marsh, P and Phillips, D (1986) *In and Out of Care*. Batsford/British Agencies for Adoption and Fostering.

Fox Harding, LM (1991) *Perspectives in Child Care Policy*. London: Longmans.

Frame, L, Berrick, JD and Brodowski, ML (2000) 'Understanding reentry to out-of-home care for reunified infants', *Child Welfare*, 79, 4, 339–72.

Fraser, MW, Walton, E, Lewis, RE, Pecora, PJ and Walton, WK (1996) 'An experiment in family reunification: correlates of outcomes at one-year follow-up', *Children and Youth Services Review*, 18, 4/5, 335–61.

Fuller, T (2005) 'Child safety at reunification: a case-control study of maltreatment recurrence following return home from substitute care', *Children and Youth Services Review*, 24, 12, 1293–1306.

George, V (1970) *Foster Care: Theory and Practice.* London: Routledge & Kegan Paul.

Glisson, C, Bailey, JW and Post, JA (2000) 'Predicting the time children spend in state custody', *Social Service Review*, 74, 253–80.

Goerge, M (1990) 'The reunification process in substitute care', *Social Service Review*, 64, 422–57.

Goldstein, J, Freud, A and Solnit, A (1973) *Beyond the Best Interests of the Child.* New York: The Free Press.

Grogan-Kaylor, A (2001) 'The effect of initial placement into kinship foster care on reunification from foster care: a bivariate probit analysis', *Journal of Social Service Research*, 27, 4, 1–31.

Guo, S and Wells, K (2003) 'Research on timing of foster care outcomes: one methodological problem and approaches to its solution', *Social Service Review*, 77, 1–24.

Harris, MA and Courtney, ME (2003) 'The interaction of race, ethnicity and family structure with respect to the timing of family reunification', *Children and Youth Services Review*, 25, 5/6, 409–29.

Harwin, J, Owen, M, Locke, R and Forrester, D (2001) *Making Care Orders Work. A study of care plans and their implementation.* London: The Stationery Office.

Hensey, D, Williams, J and Rosenbloom, L (1983) 'Intervention in child abuse: experience in Liverpool', *Departmental Medicine and Child Neurology*, 25, 606–11.

Hess, PM and Folaron, G (1991) 'Ambivalences: a challenge to permanency for children', *Child Welfare*, 70, 4, 403–24.

Hess, PM and Proch, KO (1988) *Family Visiting in Out-of-Home Care.* Washington DC: Child Welfare League of America.

Hess, PM, Folaron, G and Jefferson, AB (1992) 'Effectiveness of family reunification services: an innovative evaluative model', *Social Work*, 37, 4, 304–11.

Heywood, J (1978; first published 1959) *Children in Care. The development of the service for the deprived child.* London: Routledge & Kegan Paul.

Hunt, J and Macleod, A (1999) *The Best-Laid Plans. Outcomes of judicial decisions in child protection cases.* London: The Stationery Office.

Jones, L (1998) 'The social and family correlates of successful reunification of children in foster care', *Children and Youth Services Review*, 20, 4, 305–23.

Jones, MA (1985) *A Second Chance for Families, Five Years Later: Follow-up of a program to prevent foster care.* New York: Child Welfare League of America.

Jones, MA, Neuman, R and Shyne, AW (1976) *A Second Chance for Families: Evaluation of a program to reduce foster care.* New York: Child Welfare League of America.

King, J and Taitz, L (1985) 'Catch-up growth following abuse', *Archives of Disease in Childhood*, 60, 1152–4.

Kortenkamp, K, Geen, R and Stagner, M (2004) 'The role of welfare and work in predicting foster care reunification rates for children of welfare recipients', *Children and Youth Services Review*, 26, 577–90.

Lahti, J (1982) 'A follow-up study of foster children in permanent placements', *Social Service Review*, 56, 556–71.

Landsverk, J and others (1996) 'Impact of child psychosocial functioning on reunification from out-of-home placement', *Children and Youth Services Review*, 18 4/5, 447–62.

Lewandowski, CA and Pierce, L (2002) 'Assessing the effect of family-centered out-of-home care on reunification outcomes', *Research on Social Work Practice*, 12, 2, 205–21.

Lewis, RE, Walton, E and Fraser, MW (1995) 'Examining family reunification services: a process analysis of a successful experiment', *Research on Social Work Practice*, 5, 3, 259–82.

Lu, YE, Landsverk, J, Ellis-Macleod, E, Newton, R, Ganger, W and Johnson, I (2004) 'Race, ethnicity and case outcomes in child protective services', *Children and Youth Services Review*, 26, 447–61.

Maas, HS and Engler, RE (1959) *Children in Need of Parents*. New York: Columbia University Press.

Maluccio, AN, Abramczyk, LW and Thomlison, B (1996) 'Family reunification of children in out-of-home care: research perspectives', *Children and Youth Services Review*, 18, 4/5, 287–305.

Maluccio, AN and Fein, E (1983) 'Permanency planning: a redefinition', *Child Welfare*, 62, 3, 195–201.

Maluccio, AN, Pine, BA and Warsh, R (1994) 'Protecting children by preserving their families', *Children and Youth Services Review*, 16, 5/6, 295–307.

Mason, J (1996) *Qualitative Researching*. London: Sage.

McCue Horwitz, S, Simms, MD and Farrington, R (1994) 'Impact of developmental problems on young children's exit from foster care', *Developmental and Behavioural Pediatrics*, 15, 2, 105–10.

McMurtry, S and Lie, GY (1992) 'Differential exit rates of minority children in foster care', *Social Work Research and Abstracts*, 28, 1, 42–8.

Miller, K, Fisher, PA, Fetrow, B and Jordan, K (forthcoming) 'Trouble on the journey home: reunification failures in foster care', *Children and Youth Services Review*.

Millham, S, Bullock, R, Hosie, K and Little, M (1986) *Lost in Care. The problems of maintaining links between children in care and their families*. Aldershot: Gower.

Milner, J (1987) 'An ecological perspective on children in foster care', *Child Welfare*, 66, 2, 113–23.

Minty, B (1987) *Child Care and Adult Crime*. Manchester: Manchester University Press.

National Statistics (2003) *Census 2001 National report for England and Wales*. London, The Stationery Office.

Packman, J and Hall, C (1998) *From Care to Accommodation. Support, protection and control in child care services*. London: The Stationery Office.

Pawson, R and Tilley, N (1997) *Realistic Evaluation*. London: Sage.

Petticrew, M (2001) 'Systematic reviews from astronomy to zoology: myths and misconceptions', *British Medical Journal*, 322, 98–101.

Pierce, L and Geremia, V (1999) 'Family Reunion Services: an examination of a process used to successfully reunite families', *Family Preservation Journal*, 4, 1, 13–30.

Popay, J and Dunston, R 'Protocol 2001. Implementation Process Methods Group', Campbell Collaboration. http://www.duke.edu/web/c2method/ProcImplGroup.htm.

Popay, J. and Williams, Gareth (1998) 'Rationale and standards for the systematic review of qualitative literature in health services research', *Qualitative Health Research*, 8, 3, 341–51.

Quinton, D and Rutter, M (1988) *Parenting Breakdown: The making and breaking of intergenerational links*. Aldershot: Avebury.

Quinton, D, Rushton, A, Dance, C and Mayes, D (1997) 'Contact between children placed away from home and their birth parents: research issues and evidence: research issues and evidence', *Clinical Child Psychology and Psychiatry*, 2(3), 393–413.

Rowe, J and Lambert, L (1973) *Children Who Wait*. London: Association of British Adoption Agencies.

Rowe, J, Hundleby, M and Garnett, L (1989) *Child Care Now. A survey of placement patterns*. London: British Agencies for Adoption and Fostering.

Rychetnik, L, Frommer, M, Hawe, P and Shiell, A (2002) 'Criteria for evaluating evidence on public health interventions', *Journal of Epidemiology and Community Health*, 56, 119–27.

Rzepnicki, TL, Schuerman, JR and Johnson, P 'Facing uncertainty: reuniting high-risk families', in Berrick, JD, Barth, RP and Gilbert, N (eds) (1997) *Child Welfare Research Review*, Vol. 2. New York: Columbia University Press.

Schofield, G (2005) 'The voice of the child in family placement decision-making: a developmental model', *Adoption and Fostering*, 29, 1, 29–44.

Seaberg, JR and Tolley, ES (1986) 'Predictors of length of stay in foster care', *Social Work Research and Abstracts*, 22, 3, 11–17.

Silverman, D (2000) *Doing Qualitative Research: A Practical Handbook*. London: Sage.

Sinclair, I and Gibbs, I (1998) *Children's Homes: A Study in Diversity*. Chichester: Wiley.

Sinclair, I, Baker, C, Wilson, K and Gibbs, I (2005) *Foster Children. Where they go and how they get on*. London: Jessica Kingsley Publishers.

Sinclair, R, Garnett, L and Berridge, D (1995) *Social Work and Assessment with Adolescents*. London: National Children's Bureau.

Smith, B (2003) 'How parental drug use and drug treatment compliance relate to family reunification', *Child Welfare*, 82, 3, 335–66.

Spencer, L, Ritchie, J, Lewis, J and Dillon, L (2003) *Quality in Qualitative Evaluation: A framework for assessing research evidence. Government Chief Social Researcher's Office Occasional Papers Series No.2*. London: Cabinet Office.

Stein, TJ and Gambrill, ED (1977) 'Facilitating decision-making in foster care: the Alameda Project', *Social Service Review*, September, 502–13.

Stein, TJ and Gambrill, ED (1979) 'The Alameda project: a two year report and one year follow-up', *Child Abuse and Neglect*, 3, 521–8.

Swenson, CC, Randall, J, Henggeler, SW and Ward, D (2000) 'The outcomes and costs of an interagency partnership to serve maltreated children in state custody', *Children's Services: Social Policy, Research, and Practice*, 3, 4, 191–209.

Taussig, HN, Clyman, RB and Landsverk, J (2001) 'Children who return home from foster care: a 6-year prospective study of behavioral health outcomes in adolescence', *Pediatrics*, 108, 1, 10.

Terling, T (1999) 'The efficacy of family reunification practices: reentry rates and correlates of reentry for abused and neglected children reunited with their families', *Child Abuse and Neglect*, 23, 12, 1359–70.

Testa, MF 'Kinship care in Illinois', in Berrick, JD, Barth, RP and Gilbert, N (eds) (1997) *Child Welfare Research Review*, Vol. 2. New York: Columbia University Press.

Thoburn, J (1980) *Captive Clients: Social work with families of children home on trial*. London: Routledge & Kegan Paul.

Thorpe, R (1974) 'Mum and Mrs So and So', *Social Work Today*, 4, 22, 691–96.

Turner, J (1984) 'Predictors of recidivism in foster care: exploratory models', *Social Work Research and Abstracts*, 20, 2, 15–20.

Vernon, J and Fruin, D (1986) *In Care: A study of social work decision-making*. London: HMSO.

Walton, E (1998) 'In-home family-focused reunification: a six-year follow-up of a successful experiment', *Social Work Research*, 22, 4, 205–14.

Walton, E, Fraser, MW, Lewis, RE and Pecora, PJ (1993) 'In-home family-focused reunification: an experimental study', *Child Welfare*, 72, 5, 473–87.

Ward, H, Holmes, L, Soper, J and Olsen, R (2004) *Costs and Consequences of Different Types of Child Care: Report to the Department for Education and Skills*. Loughborough: Loughborough University, Centre for Child and Family Research.

Webster, D, Shlonsky, A, Shaw, T and Brookhart, MA (2005) 'The ties that bind II: Reunification for siblings in out-of-home care using a statistical technique for examining non-independent observations', *Children and Youth Services Review*, 27, 7, 765–82.

Wells, K and Guo, S (1999) 'Reunification and reentry of foster children', *Children and Youth Services Review*, 21, 4, 273–94.

Wulczyn, F (1991) 'Caseload dynamics and foster care reentry', *Social Service Review*, 65, 133–56.

Wulczyn, F, Goerge, M, Hartnett, MA and Testa, MF 'Children in substitute care', in Testa, MF and Wulczyn, F (eds) (1980) *The State of the Child*. Chicago: Children's Policy Research Project, School of Social Service Administration, University of Chicago (cited in Wulczyn 1991).

Index

Titles in the Understanding Children's Lives series

Children and Decision Making
Ian Butler, Margaret Robinson and Lesley Scanlan
2005. ISBN 1 904787 54 1

Children's Perspectives on Believing and Belonging
Greg Smith
2005. ISBN 1 904787 53 3

Children's Understanding of their Sibling Relationships
Rosalind Edwards, Lucy Hadfield and Melanie Mauthner
2005. ISBN 1 904787 48 7

Inclusion of Disabled Children in Primary School Playgrounds
Helen Woolley with Marc Armitage, Julia Bishop, Mavis Curtis and Jane Ginsborg
2005. ISBN 1 904787 66 5

Titles in the Parenting in practice series

Monitoring and Supervision in 'Ordinary' Families
The views and experiences of young people aged 11 to 16 and their parents
Stephanie Stace and Debi Roker
2005. ISBN 1 904787 42 8

'Involved' Fathering and Child Well-being
Father's involvement with secondary school age children
Elaine Welsh, Ann Buchanan, Eirini Flouri and Jane Lewis
2004. ISBN 1 904787 24 X

Parenting Programmes and Minority Ethnic Families
Experiences and outcomes
Jane Barlow, Richard Shaw and Sarah Stewart-Brown, in conjunction with REU
2004. ISBN 1 904787 13 4

Other titles published for the Joseph Rowntree Foundation by NCB

Reuniting looked after children with their families
Nina Biehal
2006. ISBN 1 904 787 64 9

Young People, Bereavement and Loss
Disruptive Transitions?
Jane Ribbens McCarthy with Julie Jessop
2005. ISBN 1 904787 45 2

Understanding What Children Say
Children's experiences of domestic violence, parental substance misuse and parental health problems
Sarah Gorin
2004. ISBN 1 904787 12 6

It's Someone Taking a Part of You
A study of young women and sexual exploitation
Jenny J Pearce with Mary Williams and Cristina Galvin
2003. ISBN 1 900990 83 0

Listening to Young Children
The Mosaic approach
Alison Clark and Peter Moss
2001. ISBN 1 900990 62 8

To order these titles, or any other title published by NCB, call +44 (0)20 7843 6087, email booksales@ncb.org.uk or visit www.ncb-books.org.uk